Grammar Galaxy

Adventures in Language Arts

Nova

Melanie Wilson, Ph.D.
Rebecca Mueller, Illustrator

Table of Contents

A Note to Teachers

I'm passionate about language arts. I love to read, write, and speak. As a homeschooling mom, I wanted my children and my friends' children to share my passion. Over the years, I found aspects of many different curricula that clicked with my students. But I never found something that did everything I wanted a complete curriculum for elementary and middle school students to do:

- Use the most powerful medium to teach language arts: story
- Give the why of language arts to motivate students
- Teach to mastery rather than drill the same concepts year after year

I felt called to create my own fast, easy, and fun curriculum for teachers who want to see students succeed in language arts.

Grammar Galaxy: Nova is for students who have mastered the concepts taught in *Grammar Galaxy: Blue Star*. It is intended for both independent reading and as a read-aloud for a family.

When reading aloud, share the synonyms for vocabulary words given in the text. Following each story, there are questions to ask students to check for comprehension. The answers are given in the Appendix.

Students should complete the corresponding mission in the *Mission Manual* before moving on to the next story. Classroom teachers may wish to create customized missions.

I hope your students will accept the call to be guardians of Grammar Galaxy.

Melanie Wilson

P.S. I call typos Gremlins. If you or your student finds one, check the list at FunToLearnBooks.com/Gremlins. If it is not listed, contact me at grammargalaxybooks@gmail.com so I can make the correction.

A Note to Students

I need your help. Grammar Galaxy is in trouble. The Gremlin is working hard to keep kids from reading, learning new words, and spelling correctly. He also wants to keep them from writing and public speaking. He knows that if he succeeds, the English language will be weak, and life will be miserable.

Here is how you can help defeat the Gremlin. First, read each chapter in the text, paying attention to the vocabulary words that are in **bold text**. Note the synonym (word with similar meaning) that is given for each. Then make sure you can answer the discussion questions at the end of each chapter. If you can't, review the text, and if you still need help, check the Appendix at the back of the book. Finally, complete the mission in your mission manual with the same number as the chapter in this book.

I'm proud to have you join us as a guardian of the galaxy!

Melanie Wilson

Prologue

The king of Grammar Galaxy tried not to worry. He had made his three children, Kirk, Luke, and Ellen English, guardians of the galaxy. Together with the other young guardians on planet English, they had defeated the Gremlin and saved the English language many, many times. Words and punctuation marks were returned to their planetary homes, destructive laws were changed, and the kids had learned a lot about literature, grammar, and writing.

But would the Gremlin's schemes finally get the best of them? Would they eventually face a crisis they couldn't overcome with the help of *The Guide to Grammar Galaxy*? He didn't know. He asked Screen for a status report on the galaxy. All seemed well for the moment.

Unit I: Adventures in Literature

Chapter I

The king was looking forward to his yearly meeting with the head librarian of Grammar Galaxy. The two would review a report of library usage and the types of books being checked out. He anticipated that she would have good news for him.

When the king arrived at the main library branch, the head librarian greeted him warmly. "Your Highness," she said, curtsying. The king smiled and thanked her for agreeing to meet him in the library.

"This library is one of my favorite places on the planet," he explained. "Thank you for making sure we have the funding we need to keep it updated," she said **genially**. "I can't wait to show you some of the improvements we've made." The librarian took the king to the children's section of the library and showed him the new drama and craft areas. He congratulated her on making the area so appealing to children and families.

★ ★ ★ ★ ★ ★ ★ ★ ★ ★

genially – *warmly*

★ ★ ★ ★ ★ ★ ★ ★ ★ ★

The librarian then asked the king to join her in her office. She reviewed the most popular genres being checked out. Then she explained that the library was focused on getting middle schoolers reading. "Just one in five teens reads a book daily for pleasure," she said grimly. "We want to change that. Currently for fiction, our middle schoolers are checking out graphic novels, realistic fiction, fantasy and science fiction, and dystopian and horror books. We would like to expand our collection of these titles to engage more kids."

"That makes sense," the king said thoughtfully.

"I'm so glad you agree," the librarian said in a rush. "To make room for more titles, we will have to archive less-popular genres." She held her breath, waiting for the king's response.

"Archive?" the king asked to clarify.

"We would move them to storage. But don't worry!" she said, smiling. "We have no interest in destroying books. They just wouldn't be available to check out. If the books enjoyed renewed popularity, we could easily bring them back."

"Okay," the king said slowly. "Which genres would you be archiving then?"

"Well," the librarian continued, looking at her report, "literary fiction would be removed. My understanding is publishers aren't even considering these types of titles anymore."

"Do you have a list of titles included in literary fiction?" the king asked.

"Certainly," the librarian said, handing him a list.

The king scanned the list and he blanched. "There are numerous classics on this list," he said.

"I know," the librarian said sadly. "But kids aren't checking them out. They aren't checking out newer literary fiction titles, either."

"You've tried making those titles more accessible? You have them displayed in a way that kids can see them?" he asked.

"Oh, yes," the librarian said, nodding.

"I hate to ask what other genres you recommend archiving," the king said with a groan.

"Well, mysteries, historical fiction, and adventure books aren't being checked out much," she answered hesitantly.

The king stood up and leaned across the desk in an **intimidating** way. "You can't possibly be suggesting that we archive these genres!" he said, raising his voice.

The librarian's eye began to twitch. "Your Highness, it is more that I recommend expanding our collection of titles that young people will read. I love every genre!" she said pleadingly.

The king stopped and studied her face. "I know you do," he said with a sigh. "But I can't agree to archive entire genres of books. We are going to have to come up with a plan to get kids reading them."

★ ★ ★ ★ ★ ★ ★ ★ ★ ★

intimidating – *threatening*

efficacious – *successful*

★ ★ ★ ★ ★ ★ ★ ★ ★ ★

The librarian thought for a moment. "If anyone can be **efficacious** in that, you can. But you might need a little help from the guardians," she suggested.

"Yes! Indeed. I'm going to ask them straight away," he said. He thanked the librarian and walked home to collect his thoughts.

When he walked into the castle kitchen, the rest of the family was there enjoying freshly baked cookies.

"How did the meeting go?" the queen asked cheerfully.

"Oh, fine. Actually, it wasn't fine at all. We have a problem."

"What has the Gremlin done this time?" Luke asked with a mouth full of cookie. The queen chastised him, so the king was careful not to take a bite of cookie before responding.

"It's not the Gremlin. At least, I don't think it's the Gremlin. The head librarian wants to archive entire genres of books because our middle schoolers aren't reading them."

"Which genres?" the queen asked.

"Mysteries for one," the king answered.

The queen was so shocked she forgot her manners and raised her voice. "The librarian is going to archive mysteries? You won't stand for it, will you? She *has* to be working with the Gremlin."

"Dear," the king said, patting her hand to calm her. "I'm not going to archive mysteries. And no, I don't think this is the Gremlin's work, though I am sure he would be thrilled."

"Then why on English would she suggest archiving entire genres of books?" the queen asked.

"Teens and tweens aren't reading them. She believes she can make room for books they will read by archiving genres like historical fiction."

"You have got to be joking. She wants to archive historical fiction, too? I've lost my appetite," the queen said, pushing her plate away.

"Dear, I don't want you to worry about this," the king said.

"Why not? What are you going to do?" she asked in a hopeful tone.

"I don't know," he said, sighing.

"Then I'll do something," the queen said with a determined look. "I'll organize a protest. We will demand that the library keep all of our lovely genres available for checkout. I'm going to call all of my old Grammar Girls friends. And we'll need to make signs," the queen said, talking to herself.

"Oh, no. You don't want to start a conflict with the librarian. She means well," the king said, defending her.

"She means well? I can't believe my ears. As far as I'm concerned, she's an enemy of the galaxy!" the queen declared. She excused herself, saying she had a lot to do if the king wasn't going to protect books.

"Uh-oh," Luke said when she left.

"Indeed," the king said, sighing.

"What are you going to do?" Ellen asked with hands on her hips. "You don't want Mother fighting you."

"I'd much rather face the Gremlin," the king joked.

"I have an idea," Kirk said. "You know the reading program the library has each summer? What if we started a reading program for reading genres like mystery and historical fiction?"

"If we tell kids they have to read in genres they aren't as interested in, maybe they will read less," Luke wondered aloud.

"That's possible," the king said. "But what if we give them double points for reading the less popular genres?"

"That could work," Ellen said. "I think the guardians should have their own reading program. But before we put it together, I want to review genres in *The Guide to Grammar Galaxy*. If I don't remember them, maybe the guardians don't either."

"Great plan, El," Kirk said.

"You better go tell Mother we have this under control, or she will have a huge protest organized," Ellen said, smirking.

The king nodded and left to reassure his wife, while the three English children headed to the castle library. There they read about literary genres.

Literary Genres

A literary genre is a category of writing based on style, content, length, or intended audience. There is little consistency in defining genres with the popularity of genres and subgenres fluctuating. The most common fiction genres for young people are:

Graphic novels. A novel in comic-book format.

Science fiction. Any story that incorporates advanced technology. Often set in the future, where the setting is related to the plot.

Fantasy. Based on a magical, myth-based world that may resemble the Dark Ages.

Dystopian. Depicts a difficult, unjust world that is often the result of a catastrophic event like a world war.

Horror. Scary stories in which the protagonist (main character) is pursued by an evil presence or character.

Realistic fiction. Stories relevant to young people that could happen in real life.

Action-adventure. Fast-paced action in which the protagonist faces many dangers.

Mystery. Clues in the book are used to solve a crime.

Historical fiction. The historical setting is factual, but much of the story and some of the characters are fictional.

Literary fiction. This genre's books focus on theme and character development more than plot.

"Okay. We will use this information to send the guardians a mission describing the genres and rewarding them for reading books in the less popular genres," Kirk said.

"But still giving them credit for reading books in the popular genres," Ellen added.

"Right," Kirk agreed.

"We better get busy because if Mother succeeds in starting a protest, we could have a realistic horror story on our hands," Luke joked.

What does *efficacious* mean?

What is a literary genre?

Why does the head librarian want to archive some genres?

Chapter 2

The royal family took their seats at the dining room table. Their mouths watered as they inhaled the **savory** aroma coming from the kitchen.

Each family member shared the day's high and low as they waited for the food to be served.

★ ★ ★ ★ ★ ★ ★ ★ ★ ★

savory – *flavorful*

unyielding – *inflexible*

★ ★ ★ ★ ★ ★ ★ ★ ★ ★

The king said his high was hearing from the head librarian that young people were checking out more books from less popular genres. His family expressed their approval of this report.

Luke interjected that his high was reading one of those titles. "I read a *Hardy Boys* mystery. I loved it," he said, beaming.

"That's excellent, Luke," the king said. "I loved *Hardy Boys* mysteries when I was your age."

"What about your low?" Ellen asked her father.

"You don't have to share it, dear," the queen told her husband anxiously. "I don't think we need to share lows."

"No, I *do* need to share it," the king said, beginning to redden in frustration. "I hired someone to redesign the royal family website. The work isn't done to my satisfaction and now he is threatening to sue me if I don't pay. I don't care if he hires the best attorney in the galaxy. I am *not* going to pay him until he finishes the job!" he yelled, slamming his fist on the table.

Luke stared at his father's fist. "What is *that*?" he asked incredulously.

"What is what?" his father replied.

"Your hand," Luke explained, still staring. "Where did you get that?"

The king gasped when he saw that his fist was made of some sort of metal. He attempted to move his fingers, but they remained curled into an **unyielding** fist.

"The force is strong in my family," Luke said in a solemn tone. A lightsaber appeared in his right hand. He let out a shriek of surprise but quickly began wielding it from side to side. He wondered if he was dreaming.

The queen sank in her chair, appearing faint. Ellen came to attend to her.

"Mother, what do you have in your hair?" Ellen asked.

The queen reached up to find what Ellen was seeing. She untangled a small flower. "It's a violet," she said, staring at it. "How did that get there?"

Kirk jumped up and said earnestly, "One may smile, and smile, and be a villain."

Ellen responded to Kirk's *Hamlet* quote with a Joan of Arc quote, "I am not afraid...I was born to do this."

Cook then emerged from the kitchen and said seriously, "I think careful cooking is love, don't you?"

The queen nodded in agreement with the Julia Child quote, but she looked terrified.

"Are you all pulling my leg?" the king asked. In an instant, Cook and the rest of the family were pulling on the king's leg until he yelled for them to stop.

"Am I under the weather?" the king asked himself while testing the temperature of his forehead. When lightning flashed and a mist began to fall from the ceiling, he panicked.

Before he could think of something to say to correct the situation, Kirk interjected, "It's the perfect storm!" Clouds darkened and **roiled** above them.

★ ★ ★ ★ ★ ★ ★ ★ ★

roiled – *churned*

★ ★ ★ ★ ★ ★ ★ ★ ★

"Shh!" the king said. "Be as quiet as a mouse."

A mouse appeared on the dining room table and Cook fainted into the queen's arms. "You have to do something!" the queen cried to her husband.

"'Twas the night before Christmas and all through the house, not a creature was stirring, not even a mouse," the king said. Instantly, the mouse disappeared and everyone but the king appeared to be asleep.

"I have to get to the bottom of this," he said quietly, finding himself underneath the dining room table. He crawled out and asked Screen for a status report on the galaxy.

"There is nothing out of the ordinary, Sire, except the Figurative Language Festival."

"What Figurative Language Festival? Where is it?"

"It's being held in the Nonfiction Province of planet Composition, Your Highness. The most popular event of the festival is the resemblance competition."

The king groaned. "Wake up!" he said, shaking his three children. "We have a crisis—." He was about to say *on our hands* but thought better of it. "Come with me to the castle library," he said, leading the way.

When the group arrived, he read them part of the entry on figurative language from *The Guide to Grammar Galaxy*.

Figurative Language

Figurative language or figures of speech create mental images that extend beyond the literal meaning of the words used. Figurative language is unique to a culture and requires familiarity for understanding. There are several categories of figurative language with the most common being comparison or resemblance.

Similes typically compare one common feature using the words *like* or *as*. For example, *Her hands were as cold as ice*.

Metaphors are direct comparisons that do not use the words *like* or *as*. For example, *Her hands were ice*. An entire poem or story can be a metaphor.

Personification is giving human qualities to an animal or object. For example, animals or plants may speak, clouds may be angry, or stars may sing.

Idioms are expressions that mean something other than what their words indicate. For example, the saying *It costs an arm and a leg* means it's expensive, not that an arm and a leg are required for payment.

Allusion indirectly refers to books, movies, people, or events. For example, saying "To infinity and beyond" before jumping off the bed is an allusion to Buzz Lightyear in the movie *Toy Story*.

Synecdoche refers to a whole thing by referencing a part. For example, the word *suit* is used to refer to a business executive.

Metonymy is similar to synecdoche, using something closely associated to refer to the subject. For example, Hollywood is used to refer to the movie industry.

The king explained that holding the Figurative Language Festival in the Nonfiction Province was bringing these figures of speech to life.

"So, you're saying our goose is cooked," Kirk said. The king tried to stop Kirk the moment he said *goose* but couldn't speak fast enough.

Cook entered the library with a large platter. "Here is your goose!" she said cheerfully. She placed the steaming bird on a table and left.

"No one say anything you don't literally mean!" the king warned them. He stared out the window, concerned about the fear his citizens had to be experiencing.

"We need to send a mission to the guardians, don't we?" Ellen asked slowly and carefully.

"Yes. And you'll need to use the spaceporter to get to planet Composition as soon as possible. The figures of speech have to return home or life will be a—." The king stopped himself. The children nodded and got to work on a mission they called Figurative Language.

What does *unyielding* mean?

What are two types of figurative language?

Why were figures of speech coming to life?

Chapter 3

The king had planned a weekend boat tour to surprise his family. The tour would take them to several places on planet English called "hidden gems." The king hoped it would be educational and fun.

The queen was **enchanted** that the king had taken the initiative to plan the trip. But she wanted to know what **attire** was appropriate.

★ ★ ★ ★ ★ ★ ★ ★ ★ ★

enchanted – *delighted*

attire – *clothing*

★ ★ ★ ★ ★ ★ ★ ★ ★ ★

When the king confessed he didn't know, she and Ellen began researching the issue. The king urged them not to delay as they had tickets for a set departure time. The two decided on linen outfits in nautical colors, windbreakers, and sunglasses.

Luke and Kirk were more concerned with equipment. Luke asked to bring fishing gear and Kirk suggested bringing a sonar system.

"It isn't that kind of a boat tour," the king said, becoming **piqued**. He urged his family to get ready quickly and breathed a sigh of relief when they finally boarded the spacecopter.

★ ★ ★ ★ ★ ★ ★ ★ ★ ★

piqued – *annoyed*

★ ★ ★ ★ ★ ★ ★ ★ ★ ★

When the family arrived at the tour dock, they exchanged their tickets for life preservers and boarded the S.S. Grammar along with other excited families. "It's a beautiful day for a tour, isn't it?" the queen asked another mother seated near her.

"It is indeed," the woman said, smiling. "My boys are so excited."

"Mine too," the queen answered warmly.

The captain had a full, gray beard, an eye patch, and a captain's hat with a gold braid. He used a microphone to welcome everyone aboard. "The conditions are perfect for our tour. But remain seated or you can fall and hurt yourself. That's how I got this eye injury," he said, tapping his eye patch with a smirk.

Luke's eyes grew wide and he settled back into his seat. The king and queen grinned at one another.

"We'll be on our way, but remember rule number one," the captain said. "Have fun!" He strode away while the passengers chattered excitedly.

As the ride got underway, the queen closed her eyes, enjoying the sunshine and the breeze on her face. "Thank you," she murmured, snuggling close to the king.

The king hugged her back and said, "Anything for you, my queen."

The first stop on the tour was a vineyard planted along the shore. The passengers remained on the boat while a man came aboard and used the microphone. He described how he took care of the vines and worked to harvest grapes. "I love teaching people about vineyards. I have been doing it ever since I was born from my father's thigh," he said.

The passengers laughed but wondered if he was kidding.

"Thank you for your time, Dionysus," the captain said. "We have to get to our next stop."

"Ah, yes. Tell my father hello when you see him," Dionysus said, waving goodbye.

"Will do," the captain agreed.

As the boat moved away from shore, the queen asked the king about Dionysus's odd statement.

"I'm sure he meant since he was thigh high to his father as a boy," the king explained.

"Ah, yes. That makes sense," the queen said.

"Next stop, Mount Olympus!" the captain announced as they got underway.

"Mount Olympus?" the king repeated aloud.

"Anything wrong, dear?" the queen asked.

"No. But I'm not aware of a location by that name."

"I'm sure they made up names for the stops to make them sound more exciting," the queen suggested.

"I'm sure you're right," the king said, relaxing.

One of the passengers, who was using binoculars, called out, "Whale breaching on the port side!"

There was great excitement among the passengers.

"Which side is port, Father?" Luke asked.

"It's the left, but I don't think you'll see any whales," the king said, frowning.

"Why not?" Luke asked.

"We are on a river."

"What is it then?" the queen asked, pointing to something rising from the water up ahead of them.

"I have no idea," the king said, squinting and trying to make it out.

The captain said nothing but turned the boat in the direction of the object. As he did, whatever had appeared just as quickly submerged. When the boat was in the approximate location of the sighting, the captain turned off the engine.

The queen had her hand on the side of the boat and felt a vibration that soon turned into a rumble. At first she thought the captain had restarted the engine. But then a shadow crept across the boat and a woman screamed. A giant had emerged from the water—a giant holding a spear.

"You have come to my river?" he asked as an accusation.

The passengers on the boat trembled.

"I lost Attica to Athena, but this is still my kingdom." The passengers nodded in terror.

"Are you going to Mount Olympus?" Without waiting for an answer, he said cheerfully, "Tell my brother I said hello."

"Look! An eagle!" Luke cried, pointing. A winged creature was just visible in the distance.

"That's not an eagle, Luke," the king said gravely.

As the creature approached, the passengers were astonished to see that it was a horse. It hovered over them.

"Pegasus, you're slowing down in your old age," the giant teased.

The horse snorted in protest.

"We will allow these people to continue to Mount Olympus. Lead the way!" the giant commanded. The horse began flying ahead and the captain started the engine. The giant slowly sank into the water.

"These special effects are incredible!" Kirk gushed.

"I don't think these are special effects," the king said, eyes wide.

"You mean you think this is real?" Kirk asked incredulously.

"When we get to Mount Olympus, Zeus will be there. The worst thing that could happen is the captain could mention that I'm the king of this galaxy," the king explained. "It would mean war. Athena would join the battle."

"Dear, it's just entertainment," the queen said reassuringly.

"I'm pretty sure it's more than that. I fear that Greek mythology has been moved to Nonfiction Province on planet Composition," the king said with a tremor in his voice.

"So Greek mythology is coming to life?" Luke asked. When the king nodded, Luke exclaimed, "Cool!" After a moment, he asked, "What's Greek mythology?"

Normally the king would have laughed, but he was too worried. "We have to return to the castle immediately," he said. He used the spaceporter and directed his family to follow him to the library once they arrived.

He looked up Greek mythology in *The Guide to Grammar Galaxy* and read the article aloud.

Greek Mythology
Myths are the oldest form of fictional stories. They have been told and passed down to explain creation or natural events. Greek mythology is fiction about the gods and goddesses of Ancient Greece, known as the Olympians. They came to power after winning a 10-year war with the Titans. The main characters in Greek mythology frequently appear in modern literature and movies. They are: Achilles – Trojan war hero killed by an arrow to the heel

Aphrodite – goddess of love and beauty

Apollo – god of music/poetry and healing/plague; son of Zeus

Ares – god of war

Artemis – goddess of animals/hunting and girls/childbirth

Athena – goddess of war and wisdom

Chimera – fire-breathing monster that was parts lion, goat, and snake

Dionysus – god of the vineyards who spent the end of his preborn time in his father Zeus's thigh

Hades – god of the underworld; brother of Poseidon & Zeus

Hera – jealous wife of Zeus

Hercules – son of Zeus who released Prometheus and defeated many monsters

Pegasus – winged horse who defeated Chimera and was later transformed into a constellation by Zeus

Prometheus – gave fire to humans and was punished by Zeus

Poseidon – god of the sea, earthquakes, and horses; brother of Zeus & Hades

Zeus – king of the gods; god of the sky

Romans also had gods and goddesses and combined many of them with their Greek counterparts. For example, Jupiter is the name of the king of the gods in Roman mythology, rather than Zeus.

"What kinds of things did the Greek gods do?" Luke asked. "I don't know whether to feel sorry for the people still on the boat tour or jealous of them!" he joked.

The king thought a moment. "The first order of business is to get Greek mythology out of Nonfiction Province. But I can see from your response that I haven't given you a good education in mythology. One reason is that many of the stories aren't appropriate for young guardians. I won't use that as an excuse any longer.

"I want you three to send a mission on Greek mythology before you leave for planet Composition. We'll have the guardians read some myths and help you identify characters that belong in Fiction Province. They'll need to act quickly. I don't want Zeus declaring war with me!"

The children agreed and worked on the mission with their father's help.

 What does *piqued* mean?

What are myths?

Why did people on the boat tour see what they thought were amazing special effects?

Chapter 4

The children were **abuzz** at breakfast as they discussed their upcoming writing class. Bestselling horror author Stephen Ring would be teaching students about story arcs.

★ ★ ★ ★ ★ ★ ★ ★ ★ ★

abuzz – *lively*

aspiring – *wannabe*

★ ★ ★ ★ ★ ★ ★ ★ ★ ★

Some parents, including the king and queen, had been concerned about the content of the class. But Ring's publicist had assured them that the class would not include horror or adult content. Parents' desire for their children to learn writing from a famous author had trumped their worries, and the class sold out within hours.

"I wish I could join you at class today," the king said sadly.

"Many **aspiring** authors wanted to take the class, but it was limited to students. Ask me how I know," the queen joked.

"If he's not going to share scary stuff, why is everyone excited about the class?" Luke asked.

"He is a master of his craft, Luke. Pay attention to what he shares, and your writing is bound to improve," the king said.

"May I read one of his books then?" Luke asked.

"No," the king and queen said simultaneously. The whole family laughed.

The auditorium was filled with students eager to see what all the fuss was about. They didn't know much about Stephen Ring, but their parents did. Their parents had made them promise to share details about the famed author. They applauded heartily after his introduction.

When Mr. Ring took the podium, he said, "I want to get this out of the way before we get started learning about story arcs. Boo!" he yelled. A couple of students screamed and then the auditorium erupted with laughter.

"Now that I've scared you and have your attention, I want to teach you the secret of my success. But it's not really a secret at all. Each of my books follows what's called a story arc. You know what a plot is, yes? In essence, a plot is what happens. A story or narrative arc is the sequence of events in the plot."

He began writing on a tablet while his notes were displayed on a large screen behind him. "Think of a story arc like a three-act play. In Act One, you introduce the setting, characters, and the potential for conflict. We also call this the exposition that moves into rising action. In Act Two, the conflict builds to a point of climax, where the problem is at its worst. In Act Three, you have falling action and the problem is resolved. This is also called the denouement, which is French for untying."

He held up a book. "This is my new book, but the story arc isn't new. Story arcs are ancient. You may hear them called archetypal. That means that the same basic storylines keep recurring in literature."

The author put the book down and smiled. "How many of your parents wanted to come to this class with you?" Hands shot up around the auditorium. He chuckled. "That's what I thought. Whether they are aspiring authors or not, I've found that most of them want to hear my rags-to-riches story. That's a common story arc. It's also called a Cinderella story.

"I wrote short stories when I was getting started—not novels. And that's how you should start, too. I was so broke that I had to wait until I was paid for a short story to pay off a traffic ticket.

"Later I wrote a short story about a teen girl that I thought was no good. I threw it in the trash. But my wife encouraged me to keep working on it and develop it into a novel.

"When I finished it, I submitted it to no fewer than 30 publishers that rejected it. It appeared my wife was wrong, and the story belonged in the trash after all. But one day, a publisher accepted it. In its first year of publication, more than a million copies of the book were sold. I went from having no money to pay a traffic ticket to being able to buy a dream house. That is my Cinderella story."

The children clapped and he bowed his head humbly. When the applause ended, he said, "The moral of the story is to keep writing. The rags-to-riches story arc is a popular one. But let's discuss others that can form the basis of your next writing project."

He prepared to make more notes when an immense creature emerged from stage right. It walked slowly on large, padded paws toward Mr. Ring. Its eyes were narrowed in anger. Several children screamed.

"I thought he wasn't going to do anything horror-related," one chaperone said to another, who shrugged and stared at the beast in amazement.

The lion head of the beast roared, and the sound reverberated throughout the auditorium. The **ensuing** silence allowed the hissing of the beast's snake tail to be audible. "You're good," Mr. Ring said, laughing. "I was almost scared."

★ ★ ★ ★ ★ ★ ★ ★ ★ ★

ensuing – *following*

★ ★ ★ ★ ★ ★ ★ ★ ★ ★

The goat head part of the beast stared icily at the author. "But I can use this fantastic prank to tell you about another common story ark—overcoming the monster," the author continued, trying to ignore the beast. The lion's mouth shot forth flames that just missed the author's head.

Mr. Ring shrieked and ran to the other side of the stage. "Okay. You got me," he said, trembling. "Turn the thing off."

But the children and the few adults in the room looked at one another helplessly. When the beast roared again and looked ready to pounce on students in the front rows, children began streaming from the auditorium in a panic.

Once outside, the royal English children discussed what happened.

"That was so cool!" Luke enthused.

"I'm pretty sure that was a chimera," Kirk said wonderingly.

"He's a good actor!" Ellen said.

"What do you mean?" Kirk asked.

"I mean, he obviously set the whole thing up."

"I don't think so. He seemed really scared," Kirk said. "In fact, I think the Gremlin's involved." When his siblings seemed confused, he suggested they return to the castle immediately. "It's not safe to have a chimera on the loose," he added.

Once home, the three children explained to their parents (and Cook, who was eager to hear) what had happened with the author and the chimera.

"Could you have forgotten the chimera from Greek mythology in Nonfiction Province?" the king asked.

The three English children looked at one another. "It's possible," Kirk said, shoulders sagging.

"I hope that's all it is," the king said, stroking his beard.

"What more could there be?" Kirk asked.

"What was Mr. Ring teaching you when the chimera appeared?"

"He was telling us about story arcs," Ellen said. "He explained rags-to-riches and then started on overcoming-the-monster."

"Hm. The Gremlin knew today's topic was story arcs. I'm afraid he has somehow moved them to Nonfiction Province. You are going to have to send out an emergency mission. We have to get these fictional plots and characters back where they belong," the king said.

"Could we contact Mr. Ring and ask him about the other story arcs he was going to discuss? Then we can include them in the mission," Kirk suggested.

The king thought it was a brilliant idea. He contacted Mr. Ring, explained their theory of what happened, and assured him that the guardians would return the chimera to Fiction Province at once. The author agreed to help create a mission on story arcs for the guardians.

What does *ensuing* mean?

What is a story arc?

Why did a chimera appear on stage?

Chapter 5

"This is clearly an attempt to **undermine** me," the king said, throwing the newspaper down in disgust.

"Now what, dear?" the queen asked, looking up from her tablet.

"The Gremlin wrote a letter to the editor, claiming he has changed." When the queen seemed intrigued, the king said, "Oh, I promise you. He hasn't changed."

When the queen didn't readily agree, the king picked up the paper and began reading the Gremlin's letter.

★ ★ ★ ★ ★ ★ ★ ★ ★ ★

undermine – *weaken*

★ ★ ★ ★ ★ ★ ★ ★ ★ ★

Dear editor,

I have been blamed for every problem in this galaxy for years. While most of the blame rests with the king, I admit that until now, I have been responsible for some of the difficulties.

You see, I thought that the king's approach to maintaining a strong galaxy was wrong. He is about tradition and rules and playing it safe, while I have believed that progress and flexibility are the only ways to ensure our galaxy's survival. In seeking a better way, I have made some mistakes. I would argue that mistakes are a necessary part of innovation. But they were mistakes, nonetheless.

With experience, I have come to see the value of stability. Keeping some rules and traditions in place as we experiment with new ideas just makes sense. My views have changed significantly, but our king would have you believe that I am a flat, unchanging character. He believes that no matter what the **calamity**, I am at fault because of my evil intentions.

Our galaxy would be better served if the king would recognize me as a dynamic character and an ally. Like you, I am always growing and evolving. Should I be forever **maligned** for my past mistakes? Imagine Grammar Galaxy without me as your enemy. What could our young guardians accomplish with the extra time? What could we achieve together? I don't know, but I would love to discover it with you.

Sincerely,
The Gremlin

The queen dabbed at the corners of her eyes with a tissue. "That was well written," she said.

"You can't be taking him seriously!" the king said, his voice rising.

★ ★ ★ ★ ★ ★ ★ ★ ★ ★

calamity – *disaster*

maligned – *criticized*

★ ★ ★ ★ ★ ★ ★ ★ ★ ★

"Well," the queen began tentatively, "you do tend to hold grudges, dear."

"Grudges? The Gremlin has nearly succeeded in destroying the English language dozens of times, and you think this is about grudges?" The king's face was crimson with anger.

The queen trembled and stood up to leave the room. "What I think is that you are too angry to discuss this rationally. I'm going to let you calm down and think about what you said."

After she left, the king didn't know whether he should feel guilty or be even more furious. He decided to read the letter to the children. He was sure they would see what the Gremlin was trying to do.

He found Kirk, Luke, and Ellen playing a video game. They didn't appear eager to stop playing and kept stealing glances at the screen as he read them the Gremlin's letter. The king chose to ignore this.

"Can you believe it?" he asked when he had finished reading.

"Yeah, crazy," Luke said absentmindedly, picking up his remote.

30

"So, the Gremlin is on our side now? That's great!" Ellen said, hoping to appease her father.

"In recognizing him as an ally, you're sure to be chosen for the Galaxy Peace Prize," Kirk said proudly.

"I can't believe it," the king said morosely.

"I know. It's pretty incredible," Kirk said to agree with him.

The king took a deep breath so he wouldn't say something he would regret. "What I meant was," he began loudly and tersely, "I can't believe you fell for the Gremlin's trick."

The children finally gave the king their full attention. "What do you mean?" Ellen asked, trembling. She was sensitive to the fact that they'd displeased their father.

"I mean the Gremlin has not changed. You can tell he hasn't from his letter," the king said, rather loudly. When the children didn't seem to be following his reasoning, he asked them to join him in the castle library.

Once there, he read the article on character arcs from *The Guide to Grammar Galaxy*.

Character Arcs

A character arc is the change a character experiences from the beginning to the end of a story. Changes may affect a character's thinking, feelings, knowledge, abilities, traits, work, and status.

Changing characters are called **dynamic** while unchanging characters are called **flat** or **static**. There are three types of character arcs:

1. Positive change, which in the extreme may result in an ordinary person becoming a hero.

2. Negative change, which typically reflects the negative consequences of a character's choices.

3. No change, which is characteristic of some heroes and villains. Otherwise, writers usually want to avoid plots that produce static characters.

Features of the plot that contribute to a dynamic character arc include:

- a loss or failure (Max in *Where the Wild Things Are*)
- entering a new world (Dorothy in *The Wizard of Oz*)
- needs being met (rabbit in *The Velveteen Rabbit*)

"Are you saying that the Gremlin is a static character?" Ellen asked when her father finished reading.

"I suppose I am," the king said. "He is certainly a villain, and I've never seen any evidence of true change in him."

"Hm. Maybe he just hasn't had the right experiences yet," she mused.

The king sighed. "I wish I could agree, but you have given me an idea. I'd like you three to send a mission to the guardians on character arcs. That way they will understand when and why characters change. Their fictional writing should improve, too."

The three agreed and created a mission called Character Arcs.

What does *undermine* mean?

What is a plot feature that contributes to character change?

Why doesn't the king think the Gremlin has changed?

Chapter 6

"Our Grammar Guys and Girls groups are doing Greek theater!" Luke announced enthusiastically one evening.

"That is splendid!" the king enthused. "It's an ambitious project for sure."

"Yes, and Ellen will be playing Hera," Luke added.

"Ellen, congratulations! What a wonderful honor," the queen said, with pride.

"It will be fun, I think," Ellen responded humbly.

"What about you, boys?" the king asked.

"We're part of the Chorus, Father," Kirk replied.

"What a busy time it's going to be for you. There is so much to do to put on a good performance. Remember, Kirk, when you played Romeo?" the king asked.

"I do. I learned that a drama is a play and not just girls who aren't getting along," he joked.

"Hey!" Ellen objected. "I know you've had plenty of drama yourselves."

"True," Kirk admitted with a grin.

"What else do you remember?" the king asked.

"A cast is a group of actors, the set is the background, and props are the objects characters use on stage. Oh, and lines are the words in a script that the actors say."

"I remember from a mission we did that downstage means closer to the audience," Ellen said.

"Oh, yes! And stage right means the actor's right as he faces the audience," Luke said, feeling proud of himself.

"It sounds like you are well prepared for this performance," the king **enthused**.

★ ★ ★ ★ ★ ★ ★ ★ ★ ★

enthused – *raved*

★ ★ ★ ★ ★ ★ ★ ★ ★ ★

"We are just getting started," Ellen explained.

"I can't wait to see the performance!" the queen gushed.

A few weeks later, the queen asked Ellen if she had her costume for the performance yet. When Ellen said no, she asked, "Is the Grammar Girls group supplying it, though?"

"I assume they are?" Ellen said **ambiguously**.

★ ★ ★ ★ ★ ★ ★ ★ ★ ★

ambiguously – *uncertainly*

procure – *get*

★ ★ ★ ★ ★ ★ ★ ★ ★ ★

"That isn't good enough for me," the queen said tersely. "I won't be trying to **procure** a costume at the last minute." She left to call the Grammar Girls group leader.

When she returned, Ellen asked about the costume. The queen was frowning. "She said you don't need one. I assume that means she has one for you? I haven't heard you practicing your lines. Do you have them memorized?"

When Ellen said no, the queen was stunned and a little angry. "I'm surprised you would want to look foolish by not knowing your lines."

Ellen was hurt by her mother's reaction. "Our leader says we don't have to memorize them."

The queen was even more upset that the leader wasn't taking the performance seriously. If she hadn't just called her, she would tell her so. Instead, she left to talk to Kirk and Luke. Perhaps the Guys' leader was doing a better job preparing them.

"Do you have your lines memorized?" the queen asked the boys. They were playing a game together but stopped to give their full attention to her.

"No, we don't have to," Luke answered gleefully.

"I understand you are part of the chorus, but you still have to know your lines. And what about costumes? Do you know what you're wearing?" she asked.

"He hasn't said anything," Kirk said, shrugging.

The queen tried to hide her frustration. "Is there a day planned when you will be working on the set? Or is it already done?" she asked.

"I don't know," Luke answered quietly, trying to keep his mother calm.

Instead, the queen threw up her hands in frustration and left to talk with the king. She knew he would be furious, but something had to be done before this performance was an embarrassment for them all.

The king reddened in anger as he listened to his wife's report. "Isn't the performance at the end of the week?" When the queen nodded, he arranged a conference call with the leaders of Grammar Girls and Guys. The queen wanted to be included in the conversation.

The king began, "It has come to my attention that you do not have some important things prepared for your performance this weekend. You have no costumes and no set. And my children haven't been required to memorize their lines. Are you concerned about how this is going to look?"

The leader of Grammar Girls smiled. "Your Majesty, my apologies. I should have explained to the girls that we weren't doing traditional Greek theater."

"You aren't?" the king asked in surprise.

"No," the leader of Grammar Guys interjected. "If I may, Your Highness, we are doing Readers Theatre."

The king tried to pretend that he knew what Readers Theatre was, but the queen saved him. "What is Readers Theatre?" she asked.

"Readers Theatre doesn't involve fancy costumes, sets, or even memorization," one of the leaders explained.

"Then why are you doing it?" the king retorted.

"Your Majesty, Readers Theatre improves reading fluency, listening skills, and confidence. And it's a powerful way to engage reluctant readers," the Girls' leader answered.

To cover his embarrassment, the king asked, "Then why haven't you done it before now?" While the leaders stuttered, the king changed his attitude. "I'm looking forward to seeing this performance. Thank you for your leadership in exposing children to a new form of theater."

The leaders were gracious in accepting his thanks and told him they looked forward to seeing him in the audience.

After ending the call, the queen said, "I still don't understand why there aren't costumes."

"Dear, let's see if Readers Theatre is in the guidebook," the king said.

The two of them went to the castle library and found an article on the subject.

Readers Theatre

Readers Theatre (RT) is a form of drama that does not require costumes, sets, or even memorization of lines. Instead, students may perform RT in:

Choral readings – a group reads lines in unison

Round-robin readings – each student reads a character's lines before passing the script to the next student

Performance – characters are assigned with name tags. Scripts may be displayed on music stands, freeing students to use gestures and facial expressions to dramatize the lines.

RT has been shown to increase reading skills and fluency as well as reading confidence.

"I'm surprised I didn't know anything about Readers Theatre," the king said.

"I'm also surprised you didn't know," the queen teased.

"I'm sure you knew all about it," the king teased back.

"No, I didn't. I'm interested to see what the children's performance is like. I have a feeling I will prefer traditional drama. But Readers Theatre is a great way to engage children who can't or won't get involved in regular theater productions. Theater can be very time-consuming."

"Indeed," the king said. "If you and I were uninformed about Readers Theatre, I'm sure other families in the galaxy are, too. I think we ought to send out a mission about it."

"That's a splendid idea! Families can do Readers Theatre with their kids. And they'll be better prepared for the upcoming performance," the queen agreed.

The two of them worked on a mission called Readers Theatre and showed it to their three guardians.

What does *procure* mean?

What is a round-robin reading in Readers Theatre?

Why was the king upset with the leaders of Grammar Girls and Grammar Guys?

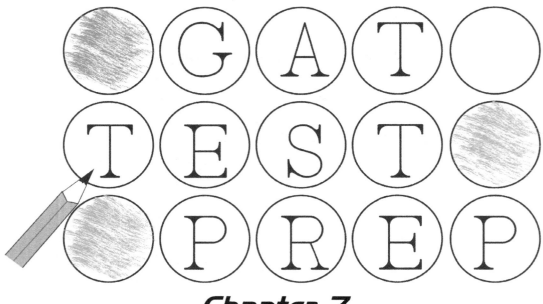

Chapter 7

Kirk joined his siblings in the media room. He had something important to discuss with them.

"The Galactic Achievement Test is coming up soon," he said.

Luke groaned.

"You know how important it is to Father that we do well on the reading section," he continued.

"Yes. And if we fail, we can forget about screen time," Luke added.

"Right. But I have some good news for you. I found a test-taking method developed by a brilliant computer programmer. It will help us ace the test this year!"

"A programmer developed a method for acing a reading test?" Luke said skeptically.

"It turns out that these tests are based on statistical probabilities and proper time usage. When you know the formula, it's easy!" Kirk crowed.

"Hm. If it's that easy, we should share the formula with the other guardians. Father will be thrilled if we all do well on the test," Ellen suggested.

"But is using this formula cheating?" Luke asked.

"Not at all. It's being smart about test-taking," Kirk answered.

"Okay. I know it's surprising that I'm asking this, but won't Father be mad if we send the guardians a mission without telling him?" Luke asked.

"Good point, Luke. What if we send it to the guardians unofficially? It's just a helpful tool in preparing for the test, and we wanted to pass it along," Kirk suggested.

"Hm. I think that would be okay. Why wouldn't Father want us to help our friends do well on the test?" Ellen asked **rhetorically**.

* * * * * * * * * *

rhetorically – *for effect*

melodramatically – *theatrically*

erudite – *intellectual*

* * * * * * * * * *

"It's agreed then," Luke said. "Show us the secret formula, Kirk," he joked.

Kirk began going over the tricks he'd learned with them. "First, you don't actually read the passage," he said **melodramatically**.

"You're kidding," Ellen said.

"No. Reading the passage wastes time. You go directly to the questions. You only have to read the passage to get the answers," Kirk explained.

"Hm. That makes sense," Luke said. "What else?"

"Look for the answer that is the most **erudite**."

"What on English does that mean?" Luke asked.

"Exactly my point. If you don't understand one of the choices, that's probably the answer."

Ellen nodded. "That makes sense. What about the formula you mentioned?" she asked.

"Right. If you don't know the answer using the other strategies, the answer is c. They have done studies, and 90% of the time c is the correct answer," Kirk said with a satisfied smile.

"But why would they make the correct answer c most of the time? Seems like an easy thing to figure out," Luke said.

"Right. That's the beauty of it. Most people won't believe c is the correct answer so often. Meanwhile, we know and can ace the test!" Kirk said, beaming.

Ellen frowned. "You're sure this isn't cheating? I don't want to cheat."

Kirk scoffed. "Of course not! This is test-taking strategy. It's being smart."

Ellen sighed in relief. "Okay. We just have to write these tips up and send them out then?"

Kirk nodded. "Father will be so pleased with our reading scores this year."

Several days later the queen received a message from a friend thanking her for the reading test tips her children had shared. "The kids are so relieved to have the formula!" she wrote.

The queen frowned. She hadn't heard about a test-taking formula or a mission being sent out. "I'm so glad it helped!" she wrote back. "Would you send me a copy of what they sent?"

The queen's friend thought it an odd request but sent her the document.

The queen thanked her and began reading the tips her children had sent out. Her eyes grew wide in dismay. She knew she had to do something in a hurry.

She gathered the children in the castle library to talk with them. By her expression, the three guardians knew they were in trouble. "I just read a copy of the test tips you sent out without your father's permission."

Kirk interjected defensively. "It's not cheating, Mother. We didn't send them out as official tips."

"You're right. You're not cheating at all. These *tips*," she said, using air quotes, "will have you all failing the test."

Ellen gasped.

"I'm thankful you didn't send them out officially, but that doesn't solve the problem. You're guardians. Everything you send is a reflection on your role. Do you understand?"

The three nodded glumly.

"I suspect that these fake tips were put together by the Gremlin. I want to give you real test-taking strategies for the reading-comprehension portion of the test. Then I will have you send them out as a mission. You'll have to apologize to the guardians and sadly, to your Father."

Ellen was near tears. She wanted to blame Kirk, but she had gone along with the plan despite knowing it wasn't right.

The queen read the article from *The Guide to Grammar Galaxy* aloud.

Reading-Comprehension Tests

Reading-comprehension tests are designed to assess your understanding of main ideas, vocabulary, and inferences. You will be asked to determine the author's purpose, to define vocabulary words from the context, and to draw conclusions based on clues in the passage.

First, read the passage before the questions. Ask yourself what the main point is as you read. The main idea is often found in the first sentence of a paragraph. Stay focused on the material by recalling related reading or experiences.

Second, note the supporting points by underlining them or making short notes next to each paragraph.

Third, read the question. Determine whether it is asking about the passage as a whole, a part of the passage, an inference (conclusion based on evidence or reason), or a vocabulary word. Predict the answer to the question before looking at the options.

Finally, choose the best answer using these guidelines:
– Choose an answer that matches your prediction.
– Eliminate answers that are obviously wrong, such as those unrelated to the passage.
– Eliminate answers that appear correct, but a detail is changed or extreme (i.e., includes *always* or *never*).
– Choose a definition for a vocabulary word based on the sentence it appears in.

"The answer isn't c most of the time then?" Luke asked.

"No," the queen said sternly.

"What do we do now that we've sent out all these false tips?" Ellen asked, fretting.

"We have to send a mission and admit to our mistake," Kirk said seriously.

"That's right," the queen agreed. She couldn't help but smile.

The three guardians sent out a mission called Reading-Comprehension Tests. They then went to explain to their father what had happened. The queen brought along a piece of his favorite pie to help him stay calm.

What does *erudite* mean?

Which should be read first in a reading-comprehension test—the passage or questions?

Why does the queen suspect the Gremlin of producing the test tips Kirk found?

Chapter 8

The royal family was gathered to watch a new TV show in the media room when a commercial started. Video of the king riding in his carriage appeared. An announcer asked in a snide tone, "Is he our king, or is he a royal pain—a leech who laps up our tax dollars to satisfy his greed? We have a monarch who is out of touch. We ride public transportation, and he parades around in a carriage."

The video switched to the king eating an ice cream cone. "While our Parliament does the real work of protecting the galaxy, our king is busy eating the profits we produce. Citizens are getting wise to his **ruse** that he is serving the galaxy."

★ ★ ★ ★ ★ ★ ★ ★ ★ ★

ruse – *scam*

archaic – *old*

dissolution – *ending*

★ ★ ★ ★ ★ ★ ★ ★ ★ ★

The scene switched to a reporter talking with people on the street. "All we've had with him in power is problems. It's been one crisis after another. I'm ready for a change, and everyone I know feels the same way," an irritable man said.

"I don't think he cares about our kids' test scores. They're not doing well, and it's all because he hangs on to these **archaic** grammar rules," a woman complained.

"Indeed," an announcer said as a bar chart appeared, "other galaxies' test scores have been superior to ours for decades. And polls show that citizens are largely in favor of the **dissolution** of the monarchy."

The queen gasped in horror. "They wouldn't do that, would they?" she asked.

The king was strangely silent.

"Father, are you okay?" Ellen asked. "It's not true what they said. Don't be upset," she said to comfort him.

"We know who's behind this ad, Father," Kirk said.

"Yes, but that doesn't mean people won't be influenced by it," the king responded sadly.

The queen collected herself. "Dear, you've been criticized many times before and you've always recovered."

"Yes, but this is something different," he said.

"It's just one commercial," she argued. "The people know you are working for their good."

The king nodded but excused himself. He was too dispirited to continue watching the show.

"It's not even true!" Luke exclaimed after his father left. "How can they say those things?"

"Unfortunately, political ads like that one don't have to be true. If the commercial was advertising a product using false claims, the commercial could be removed and the company fined or sued. Political ads are protected by our galaxy's freedom of speech," the queen said, sighing.

"You're kidding. So, there's nothing we can do?" Ellen asked.

"We can wait for this ad to become old news. People know political ads aren't truthful," the queen said with more confidence than she felt.

The next morning, the king opened his paper to see a full-page ad of himself eating a chicken leg. The photo had been altered to make him appear obese. The caption read "Let us cease to sing the praises of the English Nero. – Philipp Melanchton."

The king put the paper down in disgust and left the dining room. The queen called after him to ask what was wrong when she saw the ad. "They compared him to Henry VIII and a Roman tyrant in one quote. Clever," she said somberly.

Ellen entered the dining room and handed her mother her communicator. "My friend just sent me a picture of this billboard," she said gravely. A picture of the king was captioned: "We don't need no dictator."

"This is so wrong!" Ellen wailed.

"Yes, it's a terrible example of a double negative," the queen agreed.

"That's not what I mean! They're attacking Father," Ellen cried.

"Yes, yes, of course. There was an ad in the paper, too." The queen showed her the offensive ad.

"What are we going to do?" Ellen asked.

The queen thought a moment and said, "We're going to get the boys and have a family meeting."

Later the family met in the king's study. "We can't let them continue to spread these lies," Ellen said.

"Ellen, we live in a galaxy that has freedom of speech and freedom of the press," the king explained.

"But you're the king! Can't you order the media to stop running these ads?" Luke asked.

"And risk looking like the tyrant they're portraying me as? No. I'm afraid using propaganda is the best strategy the Gremlin has used to date. The English language will be destroyed," the king said sadly.

"What is propaganda? There must be something we can do!" Kirk protested.

The king called for *The Guide to Grammar Galaxy* to be brought to him. When it arrived, he read them the article on propaganda.

Propaganda

Propaganda is communication used to influence the beliefs and actions of an audience. It is used politically, commercially, and personally. While propaganda can be used to achieve a positive goal, it is typically viewed as a manipulative or dishonest form of persuasion.

Some of the persuasive strategies commonly used in propaganda include:

-**glittering generalities.** These vague, positive phrases are used to win an audience's support. *We will enjoy a better future for our children.*

-**name-calling.** Names that evoke strong emotions such as dictator, liar, and extremist are typically used.

-**loaded language.** Along with names, strong negative words such as *debunked*, *fraud*, and *treason* are often used to persuade. Positive words and phrases such as *customized*, *all-natural*, and *new technology* are used to sell products.

-**common people.** An appeal is made to average folk, who make up the bulk of the audience. *We don't fly in private jets, do we?*

-**bandwagon.** The audience is asked to share the opinion of experts or the majority. *Polls say people are overwhelmingly supportive of changing the law.*

-**testimonials.** Personal stories are used to persuade. *I wasn't going to vote for the governor, but she helped save my farm.*

-**association.** A positive association is made between a product or political candidate and something else. *A bodybuilder drinking a particular protein shake in a commercial associates muscle with the shake.*

-**statistics.** Graphs and specific data sets are used to prove a point. *Skydiving deaths are up 14% this year (leaving out that this is just two more deaths).*

Propaganda is a powerful form of persuasion, particularly when it's used repeatedly across multiple media formats.

To counter propaganda:

-**recognize the difference between fact and opinion.** Facts can be proven true or false, whereas opinion cannot be. A factual news article presents information without giving the journalist's opinion, while an editorial is an opinion on the news. Countering propaganda means doing thorough research and focusing on presenting facts.

-**consider the source of propaganda.** What interests, biases, and history does the source of communication have? Corporate or political affiliations can influence the information shared. To counter propaganda, clarify potential conflicts of interest of the source of propaganda. Be honest about your own.

-**quickly address propaganda for a particular audience.** Propaganda sources have biases, but so does the audience. To counter propaganda, consider the audience's most cherished beliefs and craft communication that speaks to them. A counterargument must be made quickly or you can lose audience support. For example, propaganda about what a new law will force people to do will upset an audience that cherishes freedom. Countering this type of propaganda requires a quick promise that participation is voluntary.

"We have to work quickly to counter the Gremlin's propaganda," Kirk said.

"That's right! We should use propaganda against him!" Luke said.

"No," the queen interjected. "We need to present the truth about your father and what we do as the royal family."

Ellen agreed. "Yes! We need to send out an emergency mission on propaganda," she said.

"That's a wonderful idea, Ellen," the queen said. The king nodded his approval.

The three English children began working on a mission called Propaganda, hoping that it would counter the Gremlin's ads and would cheer their father.

What does *ruse* mean?

What are glittering generalities?

Why was the king upset?

Chapter 9

"Look what just arrived!" the queen gushed. She triumphantly held up a copy of a hardcover book.

"Your book!" Ellen cried. "Lemme see, lemme see."

The queen gladly handed the book to Ellen, who immediately began paging through it while her brothers looked on.

The king hugged his wife. "I couldn't be prouder of this published author."

The queen blushed. "Thank you, dear. I couldn't have done it without you."

"All right. Let me have a look at this masterpiece," the king said to his children, holding out his hand.

Ellen handed him the book and traded places with him so she could hug her mother. "It looks amazing!" Ellen told her.

"Thank you, Ellen," she said, kissing the top of her daughter's head.

The king extended both arms to review the whole cover. *"Too Many Cooks in the Kitchen.* I love the cover," he said, smiling back over his shoulder at the queen. "And, of course, the title is **tantalizing**."

★ ★ ★ ★ ★ ★ ★ ★ ★ ★

tantalizing – *enticing*

trite – *corny*

amateur – *unprofessional*

★ ★ ★ ★ ★ ★ ★ ★ ★ ★

"Let's hope lots of readers think so," the queen said.

"You're not worried it won't sell, are you?" the king asked. "You have a good publicist."

"Not really," she answered. "I'm more concerned about the reviews. You know how mean some people can be."

"Author Terry Mark said, 'No matter how good you are, someone is always going to be against you. But never let them be the limit of your success,'" the king said kindly.

"That's a good reminder. Thank you," the queen said, hugging her husband.

"You're welcome. I'm focused on the royalty checks that should be pouring in," he joked.

The queen laughed and went to tell her friends that the book had arrived.

Several days later the queen was crestfallen when she read the review of her book in the *Grammar Gazette.*

"The queen's first book is as **trite** as we expected it to be with a title like *Too Many Cooks in the Kitchen.* The predictable plot are the mark of an **amateur** author. This 'mystery' will prove to be one too many book for your bookshelf." The review writer was listed as anonymous "to prevent backlash from the royal family."

The king had already read the review and was prepared with a pep talk for his wife, but she wouldn't listen. "I knew I had no business writing a mystery. I'm not a trained writer. What was I thinking? My poor friends will suffer through the book just to be nice," she said, her eyes welling with tears.

"Dear, I've read the book, and this review couldn't be more wrong. The characters are well rounded, the plot keeps you guessing, and the addition of Cook's recipes is ingenious," the king said.

"You have to say that," the queen joked through tears.

"You're right. I do," the king joked in return. "But I mean it. I suspect this review was written by the Gremlin."

"We can't blame every criticism of us on the Gremlin," the queen said sadly.

"No, but this is a very poorly written review. I doubt whoever wrote it even read the book. And who writes an anonymous book review anyway?" the king argued.

"That's true," the queen said slowly. Then she sighed. "But it doesn't matter. No one will read the book with this kind of review."

The king hugged her. "I don't agree with you, but I will say I'm sorry that this review upset you."

The queen appreciated his compassion and left to get more sympathy from Cook.

Then the king had an idea. He got *The Guide to Grammar Galaxy* from the castle library and looked for his children. He found them playing with Comet outside. He called them over and explained about their mother's negative book review. He then read them the article on book reviews from the guidebook.

Book Reviews

Book reviews help readers decide which titles are worth reading. A good book review:

– shares the title, author, theme (main idea/underlying meaning), and genre at the beginning of the review

– describes the author's writing style (format, vocabulary, mood)

– gives the plot of the book without spoilers (clues to plot twists or the ending)

– concludes with the reviewer's opinion of the book, the reasons for this opinion, and a recommendation for the audience to read it or not

Reviews should be well organized with the main points addressed in separate paragraphs. Supporting material should include quotes from the book or the author. To be taken seriously, reviews must include proper grammar, spelling, and vocabulary.

"Did the Gremlin follow these rules for his book review?" Luke asked.

"Come to think of it, no, not all of them," the king answered.

"We should be able to discredit his review then," Kirk said.

The king nodded. "Yes, but I think we need to do more. This isn't just about your mother's book. We need guardians to be reading book reviews so they will be motivated to keep reading excellent literature."

"This sounds like a mission to me," Ellen said with a grin.

"Should we make everyone write a positive review of Mother's book, too?" Luke asked.

The king laughed. "Uh, no. We don't want phony reviews. But we can encourage guardians to write reviews of books they love. Maybe their parents will do likewise and leave positive reviews of your mother's book."

"Let's get started," Ellen suggested. "Afterward, I'm going to help Cook make Mother's favorite dessert to cheer her up."

The boys agreed with the plan and the three of them left to create a mission called Book Reviews.

What does *trite* mean?

What do reviews need to be taken seriously?

Why does the king suspect the Gremlin wrote the review of *Too Many Cooks in the Kitchen*?

Unit II: Adventures in Spelling & Vocabulary

Chapter 10

The queen was **perusing** a magazine on her tablet when she saw an article that interested her: "100 Vocabulary Words Every Middle Schooler Should Know."

The article began with a reminder of the importance of vocabulary. "The number of words students know is **correlated** with academic achievement and even successful relationships," she read. "If your student doesn't know many of these one hundred words, success may **elude** them."

The queen agreed that vocabulary was very important. She was sure that her children knew most of the words on the list, but she wanted to test them. She left to look for Kirk, Luke, and Ellen and found them in the media room playing a game together.

"I have a little game for you," she said in a singsong voice.

"You do?" the kids responded cheerfully.

"Yes. I'm going to give you some vocabulary words, and you tell me the meaning of them," she explained.

"That's a game? It sounds like school," Luke complained.

The queen glared at him and Luke apologized.

"Okay, what does *aplomb* mean?" the queen asked.

"I know!" Ellen said. "It's a fruit. We haven't had them in a while, but I love them," she said, expecting praise.

"Uh, incorrect. But I love plums, too," the queen said, smiling at her. "Next word is *imperious*."

"Does it mean wanting to know more?" Kirk asked.

"No. Are you thinking of curious? Luke and Ellen?" the queen prompted.

Both shook their heads that they didn't know.

"Okay, how about *brandish*?" the queen asked.

"Does it mean having a popular brand name? Like you're trying to have a brand?" Ellen asked.

The queen stifled a laugh. "No, it does not. Boys?"

Kirk and Luke shrugged.

The queen sighed. "This will not do. I'm not going to tell your father that you don't know these words that every middle schooler should know."

"We're sorry, Mother," Luke said. "We're not good at this game. But we are good at Space Blaster. Want to play with us?"

"No," the queen said somberly. "This is serious, Luke. We have to know the meaning of these words to keep planet Vocabulary strong. Knowing more words means you will be able to communicate more clearly and understand what you read. When you have a larger vocabulary, you're more likely to be successful. You want to be successful, don't you?" she asked.

"Yes, of course," Luke said apologetically.

"I have to admit I haven't been using my Word Book much," Kirk said.

"And I've been using words like *good* and *bad* a lot. It's a bad habit, I guess. Oops," Ellen said.

"If you've been faltering with your vocabulary, then the other guardians probably have been, too," the queen said.

"What does *falter* mean?" Luke asked.

"It's one of the one hundred words, Luke. Before your father finds out that your vocabulary is weak, I want you three to send out a mission," the queen said. "We'll have every guardian in the galaxy knowing these words and understanding the importance of a strong vocabulary. If we don't, I fear we are on the precipice of disaster."

"Precipice?" Luke asked.

The queen sighed again. "Let's get started on the Strong Vocabulary mission and I'll teach you."

What does *elude* mean?

Why is vocabulary important?

What had led to the children's weaker vocabulary?

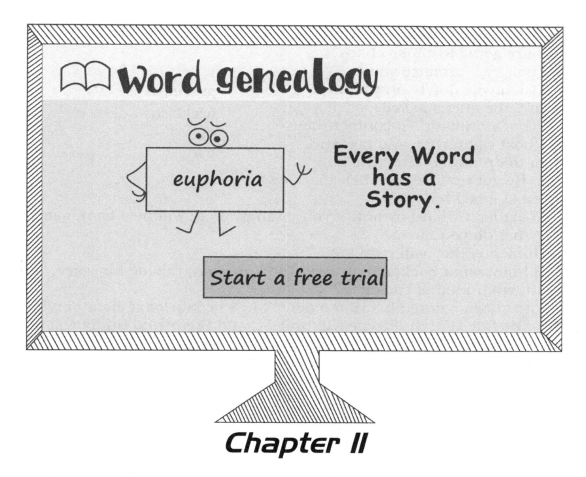

Chapter II

The king was reading the Lifestyle section of the paper when he erupted.

"Not the comma conflict again," the queen groaned.

"No, no," the king said with annoyance. "It's Prefix and Suffix."

"I thought you banished them from the galaxy," the queen said absentmindedly.

"I can't banish them. We need them!" the king said, getting agitated.

"So, what's the problem?" the queen asked.

"This article says they've started their own word-history website to compete with Word Ancestry," the king explained.

"Oh. It's always good to have competition, right?"

"No! I mean, yes. But not from those two. They have ties to the Gremlin."

"Yet you haven't banished them," the queen said.

55

The king was thoroughly exasperated. "I can't banish them! But they are going to cause chaos in this galaxy, I promise you."

★ ★ ★ ★ ★ ★ ★ ★ ★ ★

preempt – *prevent*

backlash – *counterattack*

ill – *hostile*

★ ★ ★ ★ ★ ★ ★ ★ ★ ★

"Then why don't you **preempt** them?" the queen asked.

"That's brilliant! I'll contact their web host right away and pressure them to drop their site," the king said. He got up to leave when the queen stopped him.

"That isn't what I meant. If you do that, there will be a **backlash**."

"What do you mean?"

"It means they will retaliate."

"I know what backlash means!" the king said, raising his voice. "I meant what kind of backlash?"

The queen ignored his **ill**-temper. "You'll be labeled a dictator who prevents free speech. People will protest, and Prefix and Suffix will win the people's support. Wherever their site is hosted, it will be more popular. You'll rue the day you tried to shut them down."

The king stroked his beard. "You could be right."

"I am right," the queen said smugly.

"Then what do you propose I do when those two spread misinformation about word meanings?" the king asked.

"Educate people. If they know the real meanings of prefixes, suffixes, and root words, they won't believe what they publish on their site," the queen explained.

"But what if some people still believe them?" he asked.

"More people will believe their lies if you try to shut them down. You know how people like believing in conspiracy theories."

"Hm. How about an ad campaign about their history of lying then?" the king suggested.

"You'll give them free publicity," the queen responded.

"Ugh!" the king exclaimed in frustration. Then his shoulders sagged. "You could be right," he said quietly.

"I am right," the queen said, laughing.

The king laughed, too. "We'll start with a mission for the guardians. Do you have any warnings about that?" he asked with a twinkle in his eye.

"No, that sounds like a wonderful idea," the queen said.

The king found the children and explained that they had to send out a Prefixes, Suffixes, and Root Words mission to keep the Gremlin's accomplices from wreaking havoc.

What does *preempt* mean?

Do you remember what a prefix and suffix are?

Do you agree with the queen's approach to Prefix & Suffix? Why or why not?

Chapter 12

Luke chattered with excitement as the opening ceremony for the Grammar Games began. He couldn't wait to see how he would **fare** after maturing and devoting so many hours to practice.

★ ★ ★ ★ ★ ★ ★ ★ ★ ★

fare – *do*

★ ★ ★ ★ ★ ★ ★ ★ ★ ★

He chuckled to himself, remembering the last Grammar Games he'd competed in. He had won the Better Jumper award. He didn't remember exactly what the Gremlin had done to create that problem, but now he thought it was funny. This time around, he hoped to win a gold medal in at least one event.

Kirk was coaching him again. His first event was the high jump. Kirk reminded him, "After doing the Fosbury Flop, remember to close your mouth, to roll to either side, and to cover your face if you hit the bar."

"Is that all?" Luke joked.

"You've got this, Luke. Just relax," Kirk told him.

"Were you relaxed doing this event when you competed?" he replied.

"No," Kirk admitted. They both laughed.

Luke cleared the bar on his first jump and pumped his fist in celebration. Kirk hugged him when he got off the mat. Both looked up to the stands, certain that their parents had seen the jump.

"Okay, that was great. Keep your running speed consistent the whole way," Kirk reminded him.

Luke nodded and watched the rest of the competitors. Several of them missed the first jump. That didn't mean they couldn't still win. Luke jogged in place to keep his energy high.

The height of the bar was raised. When it was his turn, Luke ran with consistent speed and cleared the bar with room to spare. Kirk was elated, and so was Luke.

"Now don't be overconfident," Kirk warned.

"What? You told me I had to be confident to do well," Luke complained.

"Yes, but not too confident," Kirk said anxiously.

Luke rolled his eyes and did squats to keep his leg muscles warm. Then he started to wonder if Kirk was right. "Do you think I can win?" he asked soberly.

"The more important question is do *you* think you can make these jumps?" Kirk responded.

Luke thought a moment. He remembered all the times he had cleared these heights in practice. Yes. He did think he could make them.

The height of the bar was raised again. When it was Luke's turn, he cleared the bar easily.

"You did it!" Kirk exclaimed.

"You say that like you're surprised," Luke responded wryly.

Kirk hung his head. "Honestly, Luke, I struggle to keep a positive attitude. You're coaching me now," he said, side hugging his brother.

In the stands, the king and queen were celebrating. "Did you see our boys hug just now?" the misty-eyed queen asked.

The **befuddled** king stopped clapping to ask what the queen was talking about. When she repeated herself, he said, "Oh, yes. Wonderful." But he was focused on how well Luke was doing.

★ ★ ★ ★ ★ ★ ★ ★ ★ ★

befuddled – *confused*

riled – *annoyed*

★ ★ ★ ★ ★ ★ ★ ★ ★ ★

Jumps continued until Luke and another boy were tied. The king knew they would keep raising the bar until only one of them cleared the height. "Let's go, Luke!" he called.

On the field, Kirk was encouraging Luke. "You've got this!" he said with confidence that inspired them both.

Luke was the first to jump. Kirk and his parents held their breath as they watched him leap over the bar that did not move.

"Yes!" Kirk yelled, looking up to his parents. They were applauding wildly.

Luke came over to Kirk and whispered, "Now we hope he misses."

"No! We hope you both do your best and you do the most best," Kirk said.

Luke wrinkled his nose. "What did you say?"

"Just focus on doing more better in the next jump," Kirk said, getting **riled**.

Luke figured the intensity of the situation was getting to Kirk. He watched closely as his competitor cleared the bar with his upper body but caught it with his foot. The bar followed him to the mat. Luke had won!

Luke shook hands with the young man and then couldn't help but leap for joy. He had just earned a gold medal in the Grammar Games!

Luke and Kirk celebrated as did the royal couple. A friend ran to give Ellen the news as she waited for her equestrian events to start.

A short time later, Luke was at the top of the awards podium. "And earning the Most Highest Jumper award is Luke English!" an announcer proclaimed enthusiastically.

"Oh, no," the king groaned. "Not this again."

"Dear, don't ruin this moment," the queen urged him.

"I'm not the one who ruined it, I can assure you," he grumbled. "The Gremlin has clearly tampered with comparatives and superlatives again."

"Does it matter, though? Look how happy our boys are," the queen said, smiling at her two sons.

"It's not the most big problem, no. Ack! Now I'm misusing them, too," the king complained. "I'm going to have Kirk and Luke help me with this before Luke's next event," he said resolutely.

The queen sighed. "I can see I won't be able to change your mind. I'm going to go watch Ellen's events."

"Our bestest hope is that we can get this matter straightened out before the awards ceremony," the king replied. "Good grammar!" he cried when he realized what he'd said.

The king found the boys on the field and explained the problem.

"I thought something was wrong," Luke said. "But they won't take away my award when we fix it, will they?"

"No, Luke. Kirk, what do you remember about comparatives and superlatives?"

"Uh, not that much," Kirk admitted.

"Okay. You two head to the library to read about Comparative Confusion. I'm going to have Screen determine what's happening to cause the problem," the king said.

In the library, the boys read the article from *The Guide to Grammar Galaxy*.

Comparative Confusion
Comparing two subjects is called a comparative and uses the word **more** or the suffix **–er** with an adjective.
He ran faster than his teammate in the 100-meter race.
Comparing more than two subjects is called a superlative and uses the word **most** or the suffix **–est** with an adjective.
He is the fastest sprinter on his team.
Add *-r* or *-st* to adjectives ending in e. For adjectives ending with one vowel and one consonant, double the consonant before adding *-er* or *-est*.
This cat is <u>nicer</u> than the other.
But the other cat is <u>bigger</u> than this one.
Some adjectives are irregular in forming the comparative or superlative. For example, good/better/best; old/older(elder)/oldest(eldest); bad/worse/worst; far/further(farther)/furthest(farthest).
Confusion occurs about when to use more/most vs. the suffix. Generally, when the adjective is a single syllable, use *–er* or *–est*. Adjectives with two syllables use either *-er/-est* or *more/most*. When in doubt, use *more/most*. The ending *y* in an adjective changes to *i* before adding the suffix. With three or more syllables, always use *more/most*. Do not use both *more/most* and the suffix.
He is quicker than he was yesterday with his math facts. (correct)
He was the most gifted pianist of his time. (correct)
She was the happiest she had ever been. (correct)
He was the most fastest runner I've ever seen. (incorrect)

When they had finished reading, the king joined them in the library. "The show *Adjectives Have Talent* is back in production. Once again we need the guardians' help in judging," the king said, out of breath from walking quickly.

"So, we need to send out a mission right away?" Luke asked.

"I'm afraid so, Luke," the king said.

"Father, could you and I send this one out so Luke can get back to the games to prepare?" Kirk asked.

"I believe we can," the king agreed, smiling at Kirk's thoughtfulness.

Luke hugged his brother and left for the competition, while Kirk and the king created a mission called Comparative Confusion.

What does *befuddled* mean?

What is wrong with Luke's Most Highest Jumper award?

When an adjective is a single syllable, which comparative and superlative should be used?

Chapter 13

The English children chatted with their friends as they waited for their first ski lesson to start. It wasn't particularly cold with the sun shining, and the snow was the perfect **consistency** for skiing. That is what the woman at the ski rental booth had said anyway.

★ ★ ★ ★ ★ ★ ★ ★ ★ ★

consistency – *texture*

★ ★ ★ ★ ★ ★ ★ ★ ★ ★

The queen looked forward to watching her children while she sat by the fire and chatted with friends. She decided to indulge in a cup of hot cocoa while she watched.

When the children were outfitted in skis and the necessary equipment, the mothers discussed how exhausting it was to get everyone dressed for skiing. The queen was surprised to learn she wasn't the only one who hadn't skied before.

"Are you going to take lessons, too?" one of her friends asked.

"I'm quite sure I would break my leg on the bunny slope," the queen joked to **raucous** laughter from the group.

★ ★ ★ ★ ★ ★ ★ ★ ★ ★

raucous – *loud*

clamoring – *demanding*

★ ★ ★ ★ ★ ★ ★ ★ ★ ★

"Yes, and I don't care for the cold," another woman added to a chorus of agreement.

"We'll let them learn while we have fun visiting then," the queen said.

From a large window, the women could see the children making their first attempts at skiing. The women initially stifled laughs as they witnessed wipeouts, for fear of offending the child's mother. But soon they realized that even the mothers were laughing. They had a great time giggling but hoped their children were enjoying themselves, too.

After some time, Luke skied down the small incline without falling. The mothers were impressed. "He has some natural talent there," one of them said.

The queen beamed with pride.

"Does the king ski?" the woman asked.

"Oh, yes. He did anyway," the queen said, wondering when the king had last skied.

At the end of the lesson, a boisterous group of beginning skiers entered the building, **clamoring** for hot chocolate.

When the English children returned home, the king wanted to hear all about the lesson.

"It was so terrible!" Ellen gushed.

The queen was shocked. "You didn't tell me you thought it was amazing."

The king stared at them both. "So it was terrible or amazing?" he asked.

"Yes!" they answered in unison.

"All right then," the king said, shaking his head. "I'll ask the boys. How was skiing?"

"It wasn't as hot as I thought it would be. I was quite frosty by the end of the lesson," Kirk said.

"That's odd," the king said. "It was a nice day for skiing, yes?"

"No," Kirk answered.

"You must not have done well. You have to be patient, Kirk. Skiing is a skill that takes lots of practice," the king said.

"Well, everyone said I was skiing like a beginner right away!" Luke boasted.

"And you're proud of that?" the king asked. Turning to the queen, he asked, "Did he hit his head?"

"No, everyone said he skiied like a beginner," the queen said.

"Ah, so they were impressed that he was skiing so well his first time out?"

"No, they were embarrassed," the queen said with effort. "That is not what I meant to say. But it's like I can't help it."

"How ordinary," the king said. "Oh, no. Now I'm doing it. Something has to be right. Screen," the king commanded, "give me a report on planet Vocabulary."

Screen replied, "The Thesaurus Office had a news conference today. They said they are beginning a new unity initiative in Synonym City. Words no longer have to have the same meaning to be considered synonyms."

"That's not old!" the king said. "They did this in the future. Ack! I'm saying the opposite of what I mean."

The king asked the butler to bring him a copy of *The Guide to Grammar Galaxy*. "We need to ignore this article on synonyms and antonyms," he said, disgusted when he heard his own words. "You know what I mean."

Synonyms & Antonyms

Synonyms are words with the same or nearly the same meaning. Synonyms are used to keep writing from becoming repetitive. For example, words like *huge*, *enormous*, and *gargantuan* can be used in place of *big*.

A thesaurus is a book or digital reference that provides synonyms for words as well as antonyms. Antonyms are words with opposite meanings. *Tiny, small*, and *little* are antonyms for *big*.

"What do we do now?" Luke asked.

"You have to go to Synonym City and make sure that words with similar meanings are together. The unity initiative is causing peace, so I'm going to make sure the director of the Thesaurus Office is retained," the king said, shaking his head as he heard himself.

"That made no sense, but we know what you mean," Kirk said.

The three English children worked on a mission called Synonyms and Antonyms and left for Synonym City. The king contacted the Thesaurus Office and hoped he would be able to say what he meant.

What does *raucous* mean?

Why is it important to have synonyms?

What was the king planning to say to the director of the Thesaurus Office?

Chapter 14

"I'm excited for a new season of *The Galaxy Has Talent*. It starts tonight!" Ellen said at dinner.

"Cook, are you going to watch with us?" the king called out. He chuckled as he knew she was listening at the door.

"If I have time after washing all your dessert dishes," she quipped.

"Ooh, good one," Luke said, looking quickly to his father to make sure it was okay. Everyone including the king laughed.

The family and Cook were interested in the new judge for the season. "Who is he?" the king asked. No one knew. "Odd that they chose someone who isn't well known."

The show started with a singer who wowed the crowd. "She's good," Cook said. "Had me tearing up." Ellen rubbed her arm in empathy.

The next act was a man in a chicken suit who told corny jokes. No one was surprised when he was voted out.

When a group of acrobats walked onto the stage, Luke pointed at them. "They're the people from the circus. TBD if they're good enough to win."

"What did you say?" the queen asked him. But Ellen interrupted, saying she was trying to hear the group's story.

"We are Acronym. We are F-I-S-H in acrobatics, and now we have some P-A-N-S to show you," the female leader of the group told the judges.

"I'm not the best speller, but are they going to fry fish for their act?" Luke asked.

Ellen hushed him.

The new judge asked if they had other employment.

"Could you repeat the question?" the leader asked. "We are ESL speakers."

The new judge said, "Forget that question. I want to know if you're single," he said flirtatiously.

"That's NOYB," she said in a **coy** manner. But she seemed to enjoy the attention.

The judge laughed and then asked earnestly, "Why are you on *The Galaxy Has Talent*?"

★ ★ ★ ★ ★ ★ ★ ★ ★ ★

coy – *bashful*

suspended – *hung*

precarious – *dangerous*

★ ★ ★ ★ ★ ★ ★ ★ ★ ★

"In an assessment of our S-W-O-T, we concluded that Y-O-L-O. AT the E-O-D, we want to know we've given our best," she said to applause from the crowd.

"Let's see what you do," the judge said with an encouraging smile.

The group moved backstage and climbed ladders or got onto rings that were **suspended** from the ceiling. Their act had the audience gasping at their **precarious** positions. But they also whispered to themselves about the letter signs that were mysteriously produced. What did the messages mean?

"What does O-S-H-A mean?" Cook asked.

"I-D-K," the king answered.

Before the act was over, the new judge had pressed the golden buzzer. The act calling itself Acronym had made it to the finals.

"The group is D-O-A at the finals. But we have to get them disqualified before then," the king said irritably. When the family asked why, he said, "Don't you hear us? We're using all these acronyms. I don't even know what they all mean!"

"What's an acronym again?" Luke asked.

The king sighed and asked that the guidebook be brought to the media room. When it arrived, he read them the article on acronyms.

Acronyms
Acro is Greek for highest point, top, or outermost. *Nym* is Greek for name or word. Acronyms are words made up of the first letter of words in a phrase. Acronyms are a form of abbreviation or shortened form of a word. Using them can lead to confusion if they aren't widely recognized. Many state abbreviations are acronyms, like NY for New York. Some countries are also abbreviated with an acronym, such as USA for United States of America.

New acronyms have developed as a result of text messaging. Some common texting acronyms include:

TY – thank you   BRB – be right back   YW – you're welcome
LOL – laughing out loud NP – no problem   WTG – way to go

Some other common acronyms are listed below:

BLT – bacon, lettuce, tomato sandwich   PBJ – peanut butter and jelly sandwich
DOB – date of birth   MD – medical doctor
MIA – missing in action   OTC – over the counter
CC – credit card   SOP – standard operating procedure
FYI – for your information   FAQ – frequently asked questions
ASAP – as soon as possible   R&R – rest and relaxation
TLC – tender loving care   TBD – to be determined
OJ – orange juice   SOS – save our souls

"With Acronym's popularity, it seems like we will be overusing these shortened terms," Kirk observed.

"Yes, but we can't have them disqualified. People seemed to enjoy them," Ellen said.

"What if we make sure that the guardians know the acronyms they're using? Then we won't be confused," Luke suggested.

"That's a great idea. I'm sure Acronym won't win the competition and the acronyms will be less popular. What do you think, Father?" Kirk asked.

"I'm suspicious of the new judge. I hope he doesn't help Acronym win. Then we will be O-O-L," the king said.

"I don't know what that means, but why don't we write an Acronym mission now? The competition won't be held for several weeks," Ellen said.

The king agreed with Ellen's logic and said writing the mission could wait until the show was over.

What does *precarious* mean?

What does TBD mean?

Why was the king suspicious of the new judge?

BILL ABC1

IN THE PARLIAMENT OF GRAMMAR GALAXY

Chapter 15

"Your Majesty," the Prime Minister began respectfully. "I am contacting you today because of Bill ABC1. I believe it has enough support in Parliament to pass and I'm concerned."

"All right. Tell me about the bill," the king responded.

"Parliament is concerned about a **marked** decline in spelling skills. The bill's sponsor argues that **arbitrary** spelling rules have contributed to poor spelling. If there are no rules, then everyone's spelling is correct. Your Majesty, If the bill becomes law, spelling rules will be eliminated from the English language."

★ ★ ★ ★ ★ ★ ★ ★ ★ ★

marked – *noticeable*

arbitrary – *random*

★ ★ ★ ★ ★ ★ ★ ★ ★ ★

The king's mouth hung open. "You can't be serious," he said.

"I'm afraid I am, Sire. What do you propose?" he asked, staring intently at the king.

"I propose not to pass the bill!" he said, his voice rising.

"I understand—" the Prime Minister began.

"I don't know that you do. If spelling rules are eliminated, spelling becomes chaotic," the king said.

"How do you mean?" the Prime Minister asked.

"Many words are spelled phonetically, making them simple to spell. Words like lunch, for example, which I'm looking forward to, by the way. But I **digress** from the topic. Other words aren't spelled phonetically. We need rules to remember how to spell them."

★ ★ ★ ★ ★ ★ ★ ★ ★ ★

digress – *stray*

★ ★ ★ ★ ★ ★ ★ ★ ★ ★

"But the spelling rules don't seem to be working," the Prime Minister said.

"Spelling rules are just one way of improving spelling, but they help a great deal when we remember them," the king said. Then he smiled. "You have just given me a brilliant idea. Thank you!" he said, ending the call.

The king explained the problem to the children at lunch. Then he reviewed the information on spelling rules from *The Guide to Grammar Galaxy* with them.

Spelling Rules

There are words in the English language that don't follow spelling rules. But learning spelling rules can improve spelling.

One spelling rule is sometimes called Magic E. A word or syllable that has the vowel-consonant-e pattern usually has a long vowel sound. The *e* is silent. For example, *cake, time, home*.

A second common spelling rule is that every syllable contains a vowel. For example, *table, gym, everything*.

A third common spelling rule is i before e except after c or when ei says /ay/ as in neighbor and weigh. For example, *friend, believe, relief*.

A fourth common spelling rule is that c makes the /s/ sound when followed by e, i, or y. For example, *nice, city, cynic*.

A fifth common spelling rule is to double final consonants in one-syllable, short-vowel words that end in f, l, s, or z. For example, Gliding from a <u>cliff</u> is <u>bliss</u> and a <u>buzz</u> but it requires <u>skill</u>.

72

A sixth common spelling rule is the **Kitty Cat rule.** When the /k/ sound is followed by e, i, or y, it's spelled with a k. For example, *kind, cat, keep.*

A seventh common spelling rule is to use ck to spell the /k/ sound at the end of **short-vowel words.** For example, *truck* and *sick*, but not *milk* because of the consonant l.

"These rules sound familiar," Kirk said.

"They should be more than familiar, Kirk," the king said. "We have to find a way to help the guardians memorize these common spelling rules. That way, even if Parliament passes a bill to eliminate them, we'll already know them by heart."

"How can we memorize them?" Ellen asked.

"Using rhymes and stories," the queen answered.

The queen agreed to help the three of them create a mission called Spelling Rules that taught these memorization methods.

What does *arbitrary* mean?

What word uses the spelling rule **i before e except after c or when ei says /ay/ as in neighbor and weigh**?

Why does the ABC1 bill sponsor want to eliminate spelling rules?

Chapter 16

"Well done in helping to defeat bill ABC1," the king told the prime minister.

"Thank you, Your Majesty," the prime minister said humbly. Then his brow furrowed. "We won the battle, but I'm afraid we haven't won the war."

"What do you mean?" the king asked.

"A new bill has been proposed. Because spelling homophones is particularly challenging, homophones would be spelled phonetically, regardless of meaning," he explained.

"How on English will we understand what people mean then?" The king was exasperated. "Consider the word *to*. We would spell it phonetically as t-o-o, which means also or in excess. It is not the preposition *to*, nor is it the number two. How can this bill do anything but cause **bewilderment**?"

"I don't know, Sire," the prime minister said. "But I know the bill has a lot of support. I expect it will pass."

★ ★ ★ ★ ★ ★ ★ ★ ★ ★

bewilderment – *confusion*

tentatively – *hesitantly*

braced – *prepared*

★ ★ ★ ★ ★ ★ ★ ★ ★ ★

The king shook his head in disbelief. "What if I address Parliament?" he suggested.

"I don't think they're open to your view on it," the prime minister said **tentatively**. He **braced** himself for an angry response.

"Parliament isn't open to my view on this bill when it will have grave consequences?" the king repeated and then sighed. "I'll get back to you. In the meantime, see what you can do to talk sense into them."

The prime minister agreed and ended the call.

The king began pacing. "There, they're, their," he said to himself. "I suppose they would all be spelled t-h-a-r-e. What has this galaxy come to?" He decided to get the queen's input.

He found her in the sunroom, reading. She noted his expression immediately. "Now what?" she asked.

The king explained the new bill and how it would affect communication. He also noted that the prime minister didn't want him to speak to Parliament.

"Oh, dear," the queen said.

"I know," the king said, sighing.

The queen thought for a moment. "What if the bill passes? People will be so confused that they'll realize the bill is a mistake. In this case, perhaps we shouldn't try to interfere."

"But isn't it my job to protect the galaxy from bad bills like this one?" the king asked.

"It's your job to protect, yes. But even more, it's your job to teach. We always learn more from our mistakes, don't we?" the queen asked.

"Yes," the king said, nodding. "But it will be so hard to see people experiencing the consequences of this mistake."

"I understand that." The queen smiled sympathetically.

The king thought for a moment. "All right. I won't stand in the way of this terrible bill. I'll just be there to help when things fall apart," he said resolutely.

"You won't be alone. The guardians will help you," the queen reminded him.

"You're my favorite queen, you know," the king said teasingly.

The queen laughed.

A few weeks later, the homophone bill had passed, and the king was incredulous reading the paper. "Galaxy is Going Throo a Meet Shortage That is Hard to Bare," the headline read. "A meet shortage?" he said aloud. "That makes no sense. Dear, it's starting!" he called out to the queen. When she joined him, he read the article aloud.

Grocers say the new homonym bill has created an unexpected meet shortage. As meat counters were relabeled as meet counters, single shoppers thought it was the place to go to find a love interest.

One single shopper explained, "I went up to the meet counter and there he was. So cute! We started talking and we had a lot in common. Then we decided to get to know one another better over a steak dinner."

This has been the end result of a number of interactions at the meet counter, creating a shortage of what we used to spell *meat*.

"That is so sweet," the queen said. "You see! They may never have met if you had blocked this homonym bill." Before the king could protest, she said, "I'm kidding."

"I'm relieved!"

"It is sweet, though," she joked.

The butler interrupted them and announced that the prime minister was waiting to speak with the king.

When the king joined the video call, the prime minister wasted no time telling him that Parliament was ready to cancel the homophone bill.

"That's good news!" the king said, beaming.

"Yes, but there's another problem. People are more confused than ever about homophone spelling," he explained.

"Of course. I will have the guardians get to work on it. Our young people will lead the way," the king said.

"Thank you, Your Majesty!" the prime minister said with obvious relief.

The king went looking for his children. He would have them send out a Homophones mission that included the common spellings and graphics that would help people remember them.

What does *tentatively* mean in the story?

Why did the queen suggest allowing the homophone-spelling bill to pass?

Why was there a meat shortage in the galaxy?

Chapter 17

The king was reading a favorite **periodical** in the sunroom when he was particularly intrigued by an article on misspelled words.

★ ★ ★ ★ ★ ★ ★ ★ ★ ★

periodical – *publication*

★ ★ ★ ★ ★ ★ ★ ★ ★ ★

"These are the top 100 misspelled words in the galaxy," he read. He noted that the words were left misspelled on the list. He briefly wondered about the wisdom of that but moved on to other articles.

That evening, he saw that the news was promoting a story on the top 100 misspelled words as well. A reporter was interviewing the words. "How does it feel to make the top 100?" he asked *embarass.* The word said nothing, so the reporter pointed to the words *congradulate*, *privelege*, and *succesful*. "They seem very excited to be nominated to the top 100 list," he said jauntily.

"Why on English are they featuring misspelled words?" the king asked aloud. Normally, he would have been angry, but the king was tired and decided to dismiss it.

The next morning, he found the queen watching a talk show. "They're having some of the top 100 misspelled words as guests," she explained.

"Why are we bringing attention to misspelled words?" he asked.

"I suppose because they're the most popular?" the queen suggested, shrugging.

Ellen joined her parents and saw the topic being discussed on the show. "The most popular misspelled words!" she exclaimed.

"You know about them?" the king asked. "How, when I just learned which words were on the list last night?"

"We talked about them in Grammar Girls. The girl who uses the most of them in her next story wins a prize!" Ellen exclaimed.

"You mean spelling the word correctly, of course," the king stated.

"We were just told to use words from the list."

"May I see this list?" the king asked.

Ellen asked Screen to pause the talk show and produce the list she received from her Grammar Girls leader. The king stepped forward to review the words and was aghast.

"They're misspelled!" he exclaimed.

"Of course! That's why they're on the top 100 list," Ellen explained patiently.

"Let me get this straight. You're going to use as many misspelled words as possible in your story?" the king asked.

"Yes," Ellen answered.

"For what purpose?" the king asked, his voice rising.

"Dear..." the queen warned.

"I'm calm," he told the queen, who still looked concerned. "Why would you intentionally use misspelled words?" the king asked.

"To improve our spelling?" Ellen suggested.

The king sighed. "This will **solidify** the misspellings, not correct them. I'll be calling your leader to have her **clarify** that the assignment must include correctly spelled words."

★ ★ ★ ★ ★ ★ ★ ★ ★ ★

solidify – *strengthen*

clarify – *explain*

★ ★ ★ ★ ★ ★ ★ ★ ★ ★

"No, don't!" Ellen pleaded. "I'll be that girl whose father causes all the problems in the group."

The king looked to the queen for help.

"I'm afraid she's right, dear. Ellen, what about creating a mission? You could have the guardians learn to spell these words correctly," the queen said. "That way the girls would write them correctly in their stories without your father having to talk to your leader."

Ellen smiled. "I like it. You're the best!" she gushed, hugging her mother.

"What about me?" the king asked. "Don't I get a hug?"

"Nope," Ellen said teasingly.

"Do you see what you've done?" the king asked the queen lightheartedly. "She's just like you."

"I take that as a compliment," the queen said, smiling.

Ellen left to find her brothers to get their help creating a Commonly Misspelled Words mission.

What does *solidify* mean?

Why was the king concerned about misspelled words being featured in media?

What is one of the misspelled words on the top 100 list?

Chapter 18

The king urged everyone to watch a live tour of the galaxy's capital with him. "The guide is not only going to show us the Capitol building but will give us the history of capitalization," he enthused.

"We've been to the capital, Father," Luke said as a complaint. A warning look had him apologizing.

"We were there when the Capitalization Constitution was taken," Kirk recalled.

"That's right! How could I forget?" the king replied.

"We had to make all the capitalizing decisions for the galaxy. That was fun," Ellen joked.

"Do you remember all the rules you had to learn?" the queen asked.

"Not really," Ellen answered. She and the family laughed.

"Well, this will be a good review," the king said. "Shh! It's starting."

The host of the tour stood in front of a well-lit capitol building. "Long considered the most beautiful public building in the galaxy, the capitol is also home of the most important document—the Capitalization Constitution. Using this **revered** document, Supreme Court justices determine which words should be capitalized.

★ ★ ★ ★ ★ ★ ★ ★ ★ ★

revered – *respected*

★ ★ ★ ★ ★ ★ ★ ★ ★ ★

"We have a special treat for you tonight. We will be interviewing the chief justice of the court. Uhh, hold on a moment," the host said, holding his ear. "I'm getting word that we will not be interviewing the chief justice." He looked at the camera and then asked the person speaking in his ear, "What do you mean she's been abducted?"

"Abducted?" the queen gasped. The children murmured in surprise until the king quieted them.

"I apologize for relating this news so abruptly. Unfortunately, tonight's tour has been canceled. We'll be going now to *Galaxy News Tonight*."

"Thanks, Tom," the news anchor said in a somber tone. "We have just received word that the chief justice of the Supreme Court of Capitalization has in fact been abducted. The other justices have been notified and have been moved to **undisclosed** locations for their safety. We don't yet know the impact of the court **disruption** on the galaxy."

⋆ ⋆ ⋆ ⋆ ⋆ ⋆ ⋆ ⋆ ⋆ ⋆

undisclosed – *secret*

disruption – *disturbance*

⋆ ⋆ ⋆ ⋆ ⋆ ⋆ ⋆ ⋆ ⋆ ⋆

"Well, I know!" the king said to the screen. "Proper nouns will be left uncapitalized, which will confuse this galaxy."

"What are you going to do?" the queen asked.

"I'm going to find out if they have any leads on the chief justice's whereabouts," the king answered.

"What about capitalization?" Kirk asked.

"Should we get a team to steal the Constitution from the Capitol before someone else does?" Luke asked.

"No," the king said, suppressing a smile.

"When the Constitution was missing, we used information on capitalization from the guidebook to direct the guardians. We could do that again until the chief justice is safe," Ellen suggested.

"That's brilliant!" the king exclaimed. He asked that the guidebook be brought to them in the media room. He read the article on Tricky Capitalization aloud.

Tricky Capitalization

Names of people, pets, places, and things are capitalized. But some capitalization rules for proper nouns can be tricky.

People and pets. <u>People's titles are capitalized when used as a name</u>. President Lincoln is capitalized. But in the sentence *Lincoln was the 16th president.*, the word *president* is not capitalized. <u>Nicknames are capitalized</u>, such as Air Jordan. <u>Languages and nationalities are capitalized</u>. For example, French and East Indian. <u>Religions and religious terms are capitalized</u>, such as Hindu or Buddhist. *Bible* is capitalized but *biblical* is not. <u>Organizations like the Red Cross and Green Bay Packers are capitalized as are government entities like Congress.</u> <u>The part of dog or cat breeds that is derived from a proper noun is capitalized</u> and the rest is not. For example, Yorkshire terrier.

Places. Buildings with a specific name are capitalized as in the Empire State Building. The word *the* is not capitalized unless it is a required part of the name as in The Louvre Museum. Astronomical names like Neptune and Pluto are capitalized, while sun and moon generally aren't. Regions are capitalized, while directions are not. For example, *I am heading west to live in Southern California.* Streets or road names are capitalized. Cities, counties, and countries are capitalized. The words city and county are only capitalized as part of the name. For example, *I have never been to the city of New York, but I think New York City would be a great place to visit.*

Things. Days and months are capitalized, but seasons are not. For example, *I see that Friday is the first day of spring.* Events, holidays, and eras are capitalized, such as the Great Depression, the Olympic Games, and the Renaissance. Specific course names and degrees like Economics 101 and Bachelor of Arts are capitalized while subjects and majors are not (economics). Only the proper name part of a disease is capitalized, such as Alzheimer's disease. Only a specific type of plant or recipe name is capitalized. For example, Japanese maple or Grammar Galaxy grapefruit. Trademarks like Coca Cola are capitalized.

When confused about capitalization, an Internet search can help.

"Let's get a Tricky Capitalization mission out to the guardians right away," Kirk suggested. Luke and Ellen agreed.

The king left to get a status report on the missing justice.

What does *undisclosed* mean?

When are the words *city* and *county* capitalized?

What should you do when you're confused about capitalization?

Unit IV: Adventures in Grammar

Chapter 19

"Mother, have you seen my communicator?" Luke asked after breakfast.

"No. When did you have it last?" the queen asked.

"Last night I think?" Luke said uncertainly.

"Have your brother or sister call you," the queen suggested.

"Good idea! Thanks, Mother," Luke said.

Ellen appeared before he could leave. "Did you change out our toothbrushes?" she asked the queen. "Mine is missing."

"No. I probably should have, but no. When did you have it last?" the queen asked.

"That question didn't help me find my communicator and we can't call your toothbrush," Luke quipped. "Ellen, would you call me and then I'll help you find your toothbrush."

"Sure," Ellen said. "Let me get it."

While she was gone, Kirk joined his mother and brother. "It's so strange. I can't find my homework. I know it was in my room last night," he said, frowning.

"We're all missing something!" Luke declared. He proceeded to explain his missing communicator and Ellen's missing toothbrush.

"I think I know what happened to Ellen's toothbrush," Kirk said. "I found Comet chewing on mine the other day. He likes them apparently."

"I'll go look for him," Luke suggested.

Ellen returned in an irritated state. "I can't find my communicator, either!" she declared.

"I'll call it," Kirk offered. He felt around his waistband for it and came up empty. "I must have left it in my bedchamber," he said irritably. He left to retrieve it.

Luke returned and reported that he was unable to find Comet.

"I'm sure he's with Cook. He hangs around her whenever she makes eggs," the queen explained. She went to the kitchen to find her.

The queen emerged from the kitchen, clearly shaken.

"What's wrong?" Ellen asked.

"Cook is gone."

"Did you look outside? She could have taken the trash out," Ellen suggested.

"Yes, I did. She is not here. She wouldn't leave without telling me," the queen said, trembling.

"Something's wrong," Luke said. "We have to tell Father."

The rest of the family agreed. They left the dining room for the king's study.

They knocked gently at first and then more insistently. The king didn't like to be interrupted, especially when he was taking calls. But the queen felt this was an emergency worthy of his potential **wrath**.

★ ★ ★ ★ ★ ★ ★ ★ ★ ★

wrath – *anger*

ransom – *payoff*

hostage – *captive*

★ ★ ★ ★ ★ ★ ★ ★ ★ ★

The queen opened the door slowly. "Dear, I think we have a crisis. Cook and Comet are missing and—" She stopped herself when she saw that all of the king's bookcases were missing. "Now I know something is wrong!" she cried.

"Where's Father?" Ellen asked, lip trembling.

"I think it's pretty clear he's been kidnapped. We should get a call soon with the **ransom** request," Luke said. "When we do, I'll handle it. I watched a show on **hostage** negotiation. When they ask for millions of dollars, you ask 'How am I supposed to do that?'" Luke said in a rush.

"Millions of dollars?" the queen said, bursting into tears. Ellen comforted her.

"I don't think we'll be hearing from kidnappers," Kirk said.

"You don't think they're just going to, to…" the queen sobbed.

"No, no," Kirk responded. "I mean that there is something else going on. Remember the last time things started disappearing? It was because nouns were being removed from planet Sentence."

"That's right!" Luke said, suddenly encouraged. "But how did we get them back?"

"I believe Father had Grammar Patrol return them," Ellen said.

"Yes, and the guardians returned them to Person, Place, or Thing Street," Kirk added. "But there were continuing problems. Multiple singular nouns were sent to the same homes. If I can get Grammar Patrol to return the nouns to planet Sentence, we'll need the guardians to create the plural forms of the nouns."

"What are plural forms of nouns again?" Luke asked.

Kirk asked for *The Guide to Grammar Galaxy* to be brought to the study. When it arrived, he read the article on Singular and Plural Nouns aloud.

Plural Nouns

Nouns that mean only one person, place, or thing are singular. Plural nouns are words that mean more than one of these. Most nouns are made plural simply by adding –s. For example, the words *kid*, *dollar*, and *flower* are made plural by adding –s. Some nouns become plural by adding –es. These are words that end in *ch, sh, x, s,* and sometimes *o*. The words *catch, dish, box, and potato* are made plural with –es. Irregular plurals are nouns that become plural in another way.

Nouns ending in -f/-fe change the f to a v before adding -es.

leaf – leaves knife – knives calf – calves

Some nouns change vowels.

foot – feet tooth – teeth goose – geese woman – women

Some nouns change multiple letters.

die – dice mouse – mice person – people child – children

Some nouns don't change in the plural. fish deer scissors pants

Nouns ending in -us usually change to -i.

cactus – cacti fungus – fungi alumnus – alumni

 Some nouns ending in -is change to -es

crisis – crises axis – axes analysis – analyses

Add s to the noun part of the word
brothers-in-law passersby

If you aren't sure of the plural form, use a dictionary and look for the abbreviation
pl.

"I think the guardians need this review, too," Ellen said.

"Whatever you do, you need to hurry!" the queen said as she looked out the study window. "I just saw some trees disappear. This castle could be next!"

The three English children agreed to create an emergency mission called Singular and Plural Nouns for the guardians. They hoped their father, Cook, and Comet would be home soon.

What is a ransom?

Why was Ellen's toothbrush missing?

What is an irregular plural noun?

Chapter 20

"Have you three been practicing piano?" the queen asked one afternoon.

A chorus of mm-hm's met the queen.

"Okay, because I haven't been hearing you," she said as a warning.

"I'll practice right now," Luke promised.

"Wonderful," the queen said.

"I'll practice after you," Ellen added.

"Kirk?" the queen prodded.

"Right. I'll go after Ellen," Kirk said absentmindedly.

"Your father and I are paying a lot for these lessons. We expect you to practice," she said.

"Yes, Mother," Luke said, smiling sweetly. His siblings smiled and nodded, too. Luke left to begin playing.

The queen planned to check on him, but first she went to the kitchen to check in with Cook. She wanted to make sure everything was set for a small dinner party she was having the next day.

She found Cook staring into the refrigerator. "Looking for something?" the queen asked.

"Oh, you startled me," Cook said. "I was just thinking."

"I do that all the time," the queen said, smiling empathetically.

"That makes me feel better," Cook said, smiling in return. "Do you need something?" she asked.

"Not really. Just wanted to make sure we were all set for the dinner party tomorrow."

"Dinner party?" Cook asked **blankly**.

"Yes, for my high school friend and her husband who are visiting?" the queen prodded her.

★ ★ ★ ★ ★ ★ ★ ★ ★ ★

blankly – *without expression*
discomfited – *embarrassed*

★ ★ ★ ★ ★ ★ ★ ★ ★ ★

"Yes, yes, of course," Cook said. She looked at her feet and shuffled them. "What were we going to serve?" she asked, clearly **discomfited** that she didn't know.

"You said you thought chicken was always a good choice," the queen said slowly, hoping to spark her friend's memory.

"Of course! Chicken *is* always a good choice." Cook smiled broadly to reassure the queen.

"All right then. You'll be ready?" the queen asked with a bit of anxiety.

"Yes, yes. Don't worry about a thing. I want you and your friend to have a wonderful reunion."

The queen sighed with relief and left to check on Luke.

She found him sitting at the piano without moving. "That doesn't look like practice to me," the queen teased.

"Oh, hi, Mother," Luke said as though he had been in a reverie. He made no move to begin playing.

"Luke, are you going to practice?" the queen asked, her voice rising.

"Oh, yes," he said. But he didn't move.

"Luke, do you feel okay?" the queen said putting her palm to his forehead. He nodded. "Did you stay up too late?" When he didn't answer, she ordered him to his bedchamber to take a nap. "Luke English, you know you have to get your sleep. You can practice when you get up."

Luke nodded numbly and left the room.

The queen sat at the piano and looked at the music Luke had left there. She wanted to play it herself, but her hands rested on the keys immobile. It had been longer than she thought since she had played, she reasoned. Then she had an idea. She could take lessons with the kids! It would motivate them to see her practice.

She was so excited about her idea that she had to tell Cook. But first, she would tell Ellen it was her turn to practice.

She found Ellen lying on a couch in a stupor. "Ellen, it—your turn to practice," she said. She wondered why she had said it that way.

"I know, Mother," Ellen groaned.

"—you stay up late, too? Even so, I want you to practice," the queen said sternly.

"Okay," Ellen said, as though her mother's request were entirely unreasonable. The queen was more determined than ever to start piano lessons. Something had to be done to motivate the children. That reminded her to tell Cook about her idea.

She found her in the kitchen, looking into the refrigerator again. "Cook?" she asked with concern. "Everything all right?"

"I—going to see if I have what we need for dinner," she said slowly.

"For tomorrow?" the queen asked.

"I—going to make some dishes ahead of time," she said with a big yawn.

"Are you all right?" the queen asked.

"Oh, yes. I—just tired," Cook answered with a shrug.

"I know you—whip dinner up in no time tomorrow. Why not take the rest of the day off?"

Cook seemed resistant at first and then **acquiesced**. "I'll—the staff to serve leftovers," she said before she left.

★ ★ ★ ★ ★ ★ ★ ★ ★ ★

acquiesced – *agreed*

★ ★ ★ ★ ★ ★ ★ ★ ★ ★

"That—fine," she said, wondering why she was speaking strangely.

When Cook left, the queen was determined to talk to the king about her. Could her dear friend Cook be suffering from dementia? She didn't remember the dinner party and she was tired. That was so unlike her.

The king was in the castle gym, sleeping on the weight bench. The queen woke him and didn't try to hide her irritation. "Why—everyone so tired?" she said, stifling a yawn. She explained her concerns about Cook and the children.

The king rose from the bench slowly and asked her to follow him to his study. Once there, he asked Screen for a report on planet Sentence. "There—nothing noteworthy there," Screen replied.

"What—you say?" the king asked. But before Screen could repeat himself, the king asked if there were any reports about verbs.

"The Verb Freedom Act—gone into effect," he replied.

"What on English—that?" the king asked, his voice rising.

"The Verb Freedom Act allows action verbs to be inactive. It also allows linking and helping verbs to refuse to serve in sentences."

"What—that mean? When—this act passed? Never mind. This—clearly the Gremlin's work. I—get it revoked immediately. But first I—take a nap," the king said, yawning.

"No! No nap!" the queen said. "We have to get the verbs on planet Sentence motivated. The guardians have work to do."

The king agreed and joined the queen in waking the children. They took them to the castle library and read them information about verbs from *The Guide to Grammar Galaxy*.

Verbs

A verb is a word that expresses action or a state of being.

Action verbs include *go, walk, jump,* and *eat*. They are things someone or something can do.

Helping verbs give more information about the main verb, often about when action occurred. Helping verbs include forms of:

to be: am, is, are, was, were, be, being, been

to have: have, has, had

to do: do, does, did, done

conditionals: could, should would, can, shall, will, may, might, must

For example, <u>The girl was shopping with her mother.</u> The helping verb *was* shows that the main verb *shopping* occurred in the past.

Linking verbs connect nouns or pronouns to a descriptive word (adjective) or explanatory noun. The most common linking verbs are also called state-of-being verbs. They are forms of the verb **to be** (am, is, are, was, were).

Become and *seem* are always linking verbs.

The verbs *taste, smell, look, sound, feel,* and *appear* can also be linking verbs. The words connected by the inking verb are underlined in the examples below:

<u>I</u> *am* the <u>queen</u>.

<u>They</u> *seem* <u>sad</u>.

<u>It</u> *feels* <u>awful</u>.

The king also explained that they were sleepy and missing verbs because of the Verb Freedom Act. "I'm going to take a nap, I mean, take action on this terrible law immediately," the king said.

"In the meantime, we need you children to go to planet Sentence and motivate the verbs to do their jobs. You will need the guardians' help," the queen said.

"I know how to write a mission on verbs, but how can we motivate the verbs?" Ellen asked.

"I—an idea," the queen said, smiling.

What does *acquiesced* mean?

What information does a helping verb give about the main verb?

Why was everyone in the castle tired?

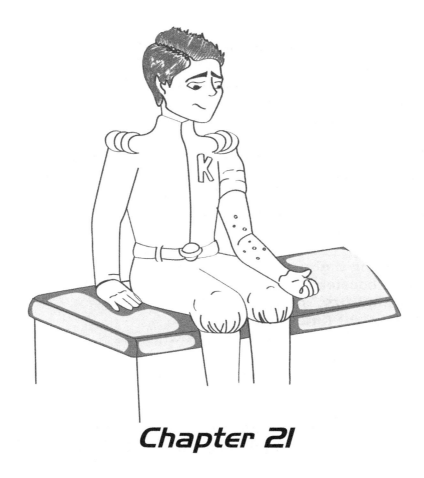

Chapter 21

At dinner one evening, the queen noticed that Kirk was unusually quiet. "Is anything wrong, Kirk?" she asked.

"No," he said. "But I am going to go to—, to—. I was up late working on a—, a—. I'm tired," he said, sighing.

"Well, I'm not happy that you stayed up late, but I'm glad you recognize that it's a problem. I hope you'll be well rested tomorrow," the queen said.

The next morning, the queen was happy to see Kirk for breakfast. "Did you sleep well?" she asked.

"No," he admitted. "I was itchy. I'm wondering if I'm allergic to the—. I use glue on my—. I have a rash," he said, rolling up his sleeve.

The queen gasped. "Is it just on your—? Do you have spots other places?" she asked.

"I don't know," Kirk said, pulling down the neck of his suit.

The queen gasped again. "You have spots on your—. I don't think this is an allergy. I'm going to have you see our physician," she said.

Later the castle doctor examined Kirk. "It appears to be the Prepositions," he said.

The queen gasped for the third time that morning. "How is that possible? When Ellen had them several years ago, Kirk and Luke memorized them."

★ ★ ★ ★ ★ ★ ★ ★ ★ ★

immunity – *protection*

sequestered– *isolated*

★ ★ ★ ★ ★ ★ ★ ★ ★ ★

"We're finding that a memorization booster is required for lasting **immunity**," he said.

"I really thought Kirk knew his prepositions," the queen said with a frown.

"I do!" Kirk insisted.

"The spots on your—, on your—. Your rash says otherwise!" the queen said crossly. Then she wondered aloud, "Why am I stuttering?"

"In my—, in my—. Mothers get upset about these things," the doctor said. "Now I'm stuttering, too. I'm sure it's just concern over a—, a—. The Prepositions could spread!" he stammered.

"Oh, dear," the queen said. "I'll have to alert the king immediately."

"What about the—, the—. It itches!" Kirk complained.

"Oh, yes. I have some lotion that you can put on the—, the—. Just apply it to relieve the itching," the doctor said.

"Thank you," Kirk said with considerable relief. The queen had Kirk **sequestered** in his room before going to speak to the king. She was nervous about how he would react to the news of a Prepositions outbreak.

"Hello, dear. How is your work going this morning?" she asked sweetly after entering his study.

"Aggravatingly," he grumbled.

"I'm sorry to hear that," the queen said. "I'll have Cook make one of your favorite—, favorite—. I'll have her make something special."

"That's nice," the king said, obviously distracted.

The queen took a deep breath. "Anyway, Kirk had a rash, so I had him see our physician." She paused until she had the king's full attention.

"And?" he asked impatiently.

"And he has the Prepositions," the queen said quickly.

"That's ridiculous. We had them memorize their prepositions when Ellen had them," the king said dismissively.

"I know. That's what I told the doctor. But he said children need a memorization booster for full—, full—," the queen stammered.

"Okay. So we need to review prepositions again. It will be okay. I can see that you're upset," the king said, standing to comfort her.

"Yes, but that doesn't explain why I'm stuttering. The word is on the tip of my—, my—, but I can't say it," the queen said. She scratched her arm.

The king noticed and asked to see her arm. After pulling up her sleeve, he confirmed what they both feared: spots.

"You don't know your prepositions?" the king asked, eyes wide.

"Of course I do!" she insisted.

The king shook his head in disbelief.

"You think I would lie to—, to—?" the queen asked with tears in her eyes.

"No, of course not," he said apologetically. "Wait. What did you say?"

"I said you think I would lie to—," the queen said, tears continuing to threaten.

"What's the preposition in that sentence?" he asked.

The queen's eyes blazed. "You're testing my grammar at a time like this?" she asked.

"No, no, not like you think," he said to calm her. "I know you know the answer. What's the preposition in 'you think I would lie to'?"

"It's obviously *to*. I hope you're happy that you've **demeaned** me," she said, covering her face with her hands.

★ ★ ★ ★ ★ ★ ★ ★ ★

demeaned – *humiliated*

★ ★ ★ ★ ★ ★ ★ ★ ★

The king embraced her tenderly. "My darling queen, I was not demeaning you. I had to prove that this is not an ordinary case of the Prepositions. It's not your fault."

"It's not?" she said, lifting her gaze to meet his.

"No. The objects of the—, of the—. Oh, no." He scratched his arm and noticed the spots there the same time as the queen. He asked Screen for a status report on planet Sentence, looking specifically at prepositions.

A video appeared on the screen with a reporter in front of a line of tour buses. "These words are touring the planet to teach others about the dangers of objectification," she said. "Their spokesperson gave us this news release. 'These words have been treated like unimportant objects of prepositions like *about, after, at, for, of,* and *to.* Until they get the respect they deserve, these words will be unavailable on Planet English.'"

"They can't possibly have enough buses for every—," the king said.

"I know what you mean. What are you going to do?" the queen asked.

"I'm going to declare a public health emergency and send those buses back," the king said firmly.

"And you'll need the guardians to help these poor objects get home," the queen said.

When the king agreed, she left to read Kirk, Luke, and Ellen information on prepositions from *The Guide to Grammar Galaxy.*

Prepositions
Prepositions show the position of something in time or space. Prepositions are combined with other words to form a prepositional phrase. A noun or pronoun, called the object of the preposition, comes at the end of the phrase. To find the object, ask *who* or *what* after the preposition.
A hot air balloon drifted <u>above the house</u>. Above what? House.
Common prepositions include aboard, about, above, across, against, along, around, amid, among, after, at, except, for, during, down, behind, below, beneath, beside, between, before, beyond, by, in, from, off, on, over, of, until, unto, upon, underneath, since, up, like, near, past, throughout, through, with, within, without, instead, toward, inside, into, and to.

"You'll need to have the guardians review their prepositions and identify objects, so they can be sent home," the queen explained.

Luke and Ellen agreed to send out the mission called Prepositions while Kirk rested.

What does *demeaned* mean?

What is an object of a preposition?

Which prepositions do you tend to forget?

Chapter 22

"Are you in a good mood?" the queen asked the king one evening at bedtime.

"Not particularly," the king joked. "But you may give it your best shot."

"What do you mean?" the queen asked, frowning.

"You're obviously going to give me a **pitch** for something you want."

The queen recoiled, hurt by his assumption.

"My dear," the king said tenderly. "Don't let my prediction of your motives keep you from sharing what you're excited about. I know you well and love you."

The queen's smile returned and she began speaking in a rush. "My friend and I were at the mall chatting and shopping when a man stopped us and asked us if we were interested in a free vacation. So, of course, we said yes. Who isn't interested in a free vacation?"

The king resisted the urge to roll his eyes. "Right. And?"

"So he explained that all we have to do is attend a two-hour presentation. You and I will listen to the talk and take a tour of their property. The resort and food are free!"

"And where is this resort?" the king asked.

"That's the best part. The hotel and property are on **Oblivion** Island. I've always wanted to go, but I've suspected and now determined that it's very expensive."

"How long is the vacation?" the king asked. "You know how busy I am."

"Yes! The travel and stay are only for a weekend," the queen explained.

"You know that the presentation will take more than two hours and will be high pressure," the king warned.

"The rep was so nice and promised that the presentation won't take long. You and I will be able to enjoy a weekend away. We can relax and can reconnect as a couple. Please?" the queen said, batting her eyes.

"When you put it that way, how can I resist?" the king said, laughing.

"Yes!" the queen said, putting her arms around his neck. "You and I are going this weekend."

"Wait a minute. Were you asking me or telling me?" the king joked.

The queen laughed.

The next morning, the queen announced the weekend getaway to the children. "Your father and I just spoke with your grandmother. She will stay with you and care for you while we are gone."

"Grandmama is coming?" Ellen asked. She looked to her brothers to see if they shared her surprise.

"She was delighted to be asked and is looking forward to it," the queen said with an encouraging smile.

"I'm not sure of that," the king mumbled.

"I'll be helping her and cooking. No worries at all," Cook called from the kitchen. She then opened the door from the kitchen and said, "The queen mother and I get along quite well."

"You get along with everyone," the king said, laughing.

"Not with you, if dinner is delayed," she joked.

The day of the royal couple's departure had the queen stressed. "Kirk, Luke, and Ellen, respect your grandmother and help her as much as you can," she said.

"Cook and I will play games and watch shows with her," Luke said.

"Uh, no. She hates games and will not watch shows," the queen said, getting concerned. "I need to give you a schedule and plan some activities."

"No, you don't," the king said rather sternly. "My mother and the children will be fine."

The queen hesitated but finally agreed.

The king's communicator buzzed.

"Don't answer that," the queen pleaded.

The king tried to resist but explained that it could be important.

"Your Majesty, Parliament and the monarchy have a problem and must act quickly," the Prime Minister said.

"Explain and do so quickly," the king said tersely.

"The outbreak of the Prepositions prompted our minister of public health to order words **quarantined** in a compound. She ordered and arranged the quarantine several days ago."

★ ★ ★ ★ ★ ★ ★ ★ ★ ★

quarantined – *isolated*

★ ★ ★ ★ ★ ★ ★ ★ ★ ★

"Prepositions were quarantined? I have not noticed nor have I heard of a problem with them," the king said.

"No, Sire. Subjects and predicates have been quarantined and prevented from leaving the compound. The result and the reason I'm contacting you is overuse of compound subjects and predicates."

"Ugh," the king sighed.

"What?" the queen asked. "Don't tell me there is a crisis and don't tell me that we can't go on the trip."

"Dear—" the king started to explain. But the queen left abruptly. She wanted to take time to cry, but she had to tell her mother-in-law that the trip was canceled.

The king asked his children to join him in the library. He asked them to be especially kind to their mother because of her disappointment. Then he read them the entry on compound subjects and predicates from *The Guide to Grammar Galaxy*.

Compound Subjects and Predicates
The **subject** of a sentence is the noun or pronoun that is doing or being. It is usually found at the beginning of a sentence. To find the subject, find the verb and ask, "Who or what?" followed by the verb.

A **simple subject** is only the noun or pronoun the sentence is about.

The complete subject includes the adjectives and article adjectives (a, an, the) that describe the subject. For example:

The five boys were terrified.

The simple subject is *boys*. The complete subject is *The five boys*.

A **predicate** is the part of the sentence that says what the subject does or is. The **complete predicate** includes the verb, adverbs, and everything besides the subject. The **simple predicate** is the verb or verb phrase. In the sentence, "The little girl

---

played with her dolls," *played with her dolls* is the complete predicate and *played* is the simple predicate. To find the predicate, ask, "What is being said about?" after the subject.

A compound subject is more than one subject with the same predicate.

The <u>boys</u> and <u>girls</u> play board games.

A compound predicate is two or more verbs with the same subject.

The boys <u>played</u> board games and <u>jumped</u> on the trampoline.

Compound subjects and predicates are combined by coordinating conjunctions (*and, or*).

"What do you and the prime minister need us to do?" Ellen asked.

"The prime minister and I need you to send out a mission and go to planet Sentence on our behalf. This quarantine and its result are making sentences lengthy and have gotten me into trouble with your mother," the king said.

"Father, you and Mother could still go on your trip. Kirk, Luke, and I can manage and we will have Grandmama here," Ellen said.

The king stroked his beard as he thought. "Your mother and I may be accused of abandoning our duties and leaving the galaxy in chaos."

"We and the guardians will complete this mission and will end the quarantine immediately. What could go wrong?" Ellen asked.

The king was wary but agreed to have the children write a mission called Compound Subjects and Predicates. He went to give his wife the good news.

What does *oblivion* mean?

What is a compound predicate?

Does the king's mother like to care for her grandchildren?

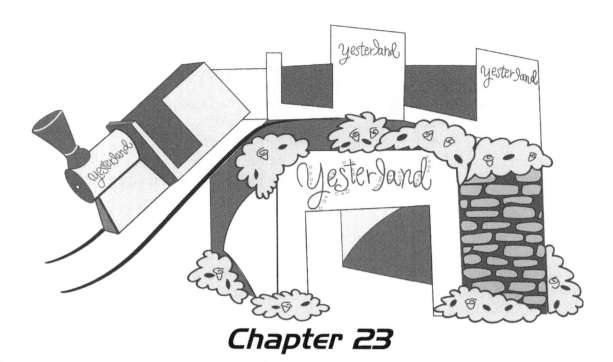

Chapter 23

"What is one of my frequent sayings?" the queen asked with a big smile at dinner.

"Are you sure your room is clean?" Luke joked.

"Yes, that is one of them," the queen said, laughing.

"Try, try again," Ellen answered.

"Yes! That's the one I was thinking of. Our trip to Yesterland wasn't great. But I think we should try again."

The rest of the family wasn't enthusiastic.

"What's wrong?" she asked, disappointment evident in her voice.

"No electronics, right?" Luke asked.

"Right. If I recall correctly, they had no electricity for charging devices," the queen admitted.

Kirk stifled a groan.

"I think a screen-free trip would do us all some good," the king said, hoping to earn his wife's favor.

"It would, and remember that there are fun rides and interesting demonstrations there. We won't even need screens," the queen said.

"Okay. Let's go. I loved the clothing," Ellen said.

"I did like the lemonade," Luke admitted.

Kirk smiled. "I don't think I'll **perish** without a screen for a few days."

The rest of the family laughed.

★ ★ ★ ★ ★ ★ ★ ★ ★ ★

perish – die

summarily – instantly

★ ★ ★ ★ ★ ★ ★ ★ ★ ★

The king's suggestion to take the carriage to Yesterland was **summarily** dismissed by the queen. "We did that last time, dear," she said firmly.

When he suggested that it had added to the fun, the rest of the family shook their heads to disagree. He grumbled, "Why would we take contemporary transportation to a historical theme park?" But he gave up the idea of taking the carriage to keep the peace.

The royal family unpacked their belongings when they checked into the rustic lodging. "This place is even more **quaint** than I remembered," the queen said with a sigh. "And I already feel less stressed." She put her arm

★ ★ ★ ★ ★ ★ ★ ★ ★ ★

quaint – old-fashioned

★ ★ ★ ★ ★ ★ ★ ★ ★ ★

around her husband's waist. "It's going to be a lovely time. Thank you for agreeing to it."

"Thank you for saying yes when I proposed years ago. I'm the luckiest king in the universe," he said, kissing the top of her head.

"Is this trip romantic? If it is, I don't think I'll like it," Luke joked.

The queen ruffled Luke's hair and said they could start making their way to the park entrance.

"May we ride the train first?" Ellen asked.

"Aww, I wanna ride something fast, not a slow train," Luke complained. "But, they only rided slow stuff in the past, right?"

"Well, yes. What did you say?" the queen asked.

The king put his hand on his wife's shoulder and took over. "Luke, slowing down is one of the reasons we are here," he explained. He smiled at his wife, hoping he had appeased her.

"That's right," she said, smiling.

The family made their way to the train station.

"My friend's family goed on this train and sayed it was fun," Ellen said, hoping to encourage Luke.

"What did you say?" the queen asked.

"The train will be fun," Ellen answered sweetly.

"Yes," the queen agreed with a smile. "I'm looking forward to it."

The royal family boarded the small train with a dozen other families. An announcer began giving them the history of trains as they left the station. "This is what's known as a steam locomotive. Fuel is burned to produce steam in a boiler. That steam moves the pistons that in turn cause the wheels to move on the track."

The announcer continued. "The first steam locomotives were built in the United Kingdom in the early 1800s. By the 1900s, the first passenger steam train reached speeds over 100 mph. That's over 160 kilometers per hour. That train was called the Flying Scotsman. This train will not be moving that fast. Sorry, kids!" he apologized.

Luke laughed and said, "Too bad." He leaned over and told his mother, "I thinked this would be boring, but it's fun."

"We leaved our screens at home but not our proper grammar," the queen replied. She gasped when she realized what she'd said. She turned to the king behind her. "I hate to say it, but something is wrong in the galaxy."

"Dear, you always worry when we go on trips. Everything is fine!" the king said, enjoying the ride.

"Okay, but when you realize I'm right, remember that I telled you," the queen said, crossing her arms.

"What did you say?" the king asked.

When the queen repeated herself, the king told his family to get off at the next stop.

"What's wrong?" Kirk asked when they were off the train.

"What happened to ruin our trip last time?" the king asked.

"Something to do with verbs," Kirk said.

"Yes, that's right. Irregular verbs. The Gremlin had authorities on planet Sentence believing that all verbs had to be treated the same," the king said, remembering. "It's happening again."

The queen felt faint and sat down on a bench.

"What are irregular verbs again?" Luke asked.

"I'll use my communicator to connect with Screen," the king said, reaching for it. "Ack! I leaved it at home."

"I have mine," Kirk admitted. "I bringed a solar power supply for it. You know, just in case."

"Kirk, you know your mother didn't want you to have screens on this trip."

"I'm sorry, Father," Kirk said, hanging his head.

"Your disobedience was beneficial this time, but that won't always be the case. Connect with Screen for me, please."

Kirk did as his father asked and was soon able to get information on irregular verbs. He read it aloud.

Irregular Verbs					
Verb tenses show when something occurred. The three tenses are **present tense** (something is occurring now), **future tense** (something will happen), and **past tense** (something has already occurred). Irregular verbs do not form the past tense using –d or –ed as other verbs do. Most irregular verbs are learned in conversation. A chart of common irregular verbs follows.					
be	**was, were**	freeze	**froze**	seek	**sought**
become	**became**	get	**got**	sell	**sold**
begin	**began**	give	**gave**	send	**sent**
blow	**blew**	go	**went**	shake	**shook**
break	**broke**	grow	**grew**	shine	**shone**
bring	**brought**	have	**had**	sing	**sang**
build	**built**	hear	**heard**	sit	**sat**
burst	**burst**	hide	**hid**	sleep	**slept**
buy	**bought**	hold	**held**	speak	**spoke**
catch	**caught**	hurt	**hurt**	spend	**spent**
choose	**chose**	keep	**kept**	spring	**sprang**
come	**came**	know	**knew**	stand	**stood**
cut	**cut**	lay	**laid**	steal	**stole**
deal	**dealt**	lead	**led**	swim	**swam**
do	**did**	leave	**left**	swing	**swung**
drink	**drank**	let	**let**	take	**took**
drive	**drove**	lie	**lay**	teach	**taught**
eat	**ate**	lose	**lost**	tear	**tore**
fall	**fell**	make	**made**	tell	**told**
feed	**fed**	meet	**met**	think	**thought**
feel	**felt**	pay	**paid**	throw	**threw**
fight	**fought**	quit	**quit**	understand	**understood**
find	**found**	read	**read**	wake	**woke**
fly	**flew**	ride	**rode**	wear	**wore**
forbid	**forbade**	run	**ran**	win	**won**

forget	**forgot**	say	**said**	write	**wrote**
forgive	**forgave**	see	**saw**		

"So, they maked it so every verb is getting a -d or -ed ending for the past tense?" Luke asked.

The king cringed at Luke's grammar but nodded.

"What do we do?"

"Don't tell me we have to end our trip again," the queen wailed.

The king seemed frustrated but then had an idea.

"No. We're going to enjoy the park. But the children will have to take some time to send out an Irregular Verbs mission using Kirk's communicator," he said.

The children got to work so they could ride the log flume.

What does *quaint* mean?

What is an example of an irregular verb?

Why didn't the queen want screens on the trip?

Chapter 24

Luke groaned about his dental appointment. "Do I have to go?" he whined.

"Only if you want to keep your teeth," the queen said **dryly**.

"It takes soooo long," he complained again.

"Okay. You don't have to go."

"I don't? What's the catch?" Luke asked suspiciously.

"No sweets for you. We can't take the chance that you'll have an untreated cavity," the queen explained solemnly.

"I knew it. No deal," he **rejoined**.

The queen smiled. "Wonderful. Now, no more complaining or you'll go without sweets as a consequence."

Luke nodded, knowing he had already been **impudent**.

★ ★ ★ ★ ★ ★ ★ ★ ★ ★

dryly – wittily

rejoined – retorted

impudent – disrespectful

★ ★ ★ ★ ★ ★ ★ ★ ★ ★

After his exam, the dentist had bad news for them. "Luke has two cavities," he announced.

The queen frowned and sighed. "But he's brushing!" she argued.

"Yes, he's brushing but not thorough," the dentist said.

The queen frowned again. The dentist mistook her expression as confusion.

"Let me show you what I mean. Using an electrically toothbrush, he needs to brush slow, like this. This circularly head is just the right size for his teeth. He also needs to floss each tooth individual," the dentist said, demonstrating.

The queen was flustered but nodded and said, "I see. Luke, you need to do a better job brushing and flossing."

Luke nodded, though his mouth was still open to the dentist.

"I'm going to send home a new brush and floss that I expect you to use frequent," the dentist said.

The queen frowned but tried to cover by smiling and nodding. "He will," she said.

"You'll also need to make an appointment so we can treat the cavities quick," the dentist said.

The queen said she would have to discuss it with her husband first.

On the way home, Luke noticed his mother's continuing upset.

"I'm sorry, Mother. I'll do a better job brushing," he said.

"I know you will," she replied, distracted.

"What's wrong?" he asked. "Are you worried that Father will be upset?"

"No. Yes! I don't know," she said, wringing her hands. "Are you comfortable with that dentist?" she asked.

"No. How can you be comfortable with a dentist?" Luke joked.

"That's not what I mean. Did you notice anything strange about him, like his grammar?" she asked.

"No. Does our dentist have to have good grammar?" he asked, surprised at the question.

"No, of course not!" she replied defensively. "Well, maybe." She sighed. "Something just seemed off."

"I do have two cavities and you know how Father is about dental expenses. You're probably just worried about that," Luke said to calm his mother.

The queen smiled gratefully. "That was quite wise, Luke. Thank you."

Luke beamed with pride.

The queen was nervous when she broke the news of the cavities to her husband.

"Isn't he brushing?" the king asked, his voice rising.

"Yes, yes, he's brushing. He just needs to do a better job. And he will need two fillings," the queen blurted out.

"How much will that be?" the king asked tersely.

"I don't know."

"You didn't ask?" the king asked incredulously.

"No. I'm not sure we want to use him," the queen replied hesitantly.

"I should have known that you would want to get the best price. I apologize for my tone, my dear," the king said.

The queen grimaced. "Actually, his grammar made me nervous."

The king stopped and stared at her. "His grammar?"

"Yes," the queen said. "He said Luke needed to floss each tooth individual."

"-ly. Individually," the king corrected.

"Right. But he said individual," the queen said.

"Hm. Should our dentist have proper grammar?" the king mused aloud.

"That's what Luke asked me," the queen said.

"Let's get his price list and then we'll decide," the king said.

Cook found them and said dinner would soon be served. "I made brisket and roasted it slow," she said proudly.

"Slowly," the king and queen said in unison.

"I made brisket and roasted it slow," Cook repeated slowly.

The queen smiled encouragingly. "We can't wait!"

When Cook left the room, the king said, "Our cook doesn't have perfect grammar. Our dentist doesn't have to, either."

"But that isn't like Cook. Something is wrong," the queen said.

"I don't suppose I can look into it after dinner?" the king asked.

When the queen shook her head, the king asked Screen for a status report on planet Sentence.

"There is nothing newsworthy to report, Your Highness," Screen said.

"You see? All is well," the king told his wife.

"However, everyone on the planet is talking about the discovery that adverbs and adjectives are identical twins separated at birth. They have traded places on the planet. Adverbs are now living near nouns, and adjectives are living near verbs," Screen continued.

"The eventually result will be disastrous," the king said, gasping when he realized his error.

"I'll get *The Guide to Grammar Galaxy* and will meet you in the dining room. The children will need to act swift," the queen said.

"-ly," the king replied. He nodded and left to gather the children for dinner.

After the family had eaten, the king and queen explained the problem on planet Sentence. The queen read the article on adjective-adverb confusion aloud.

Adjective-Adverb Confusion

Adjectives describe nouns and tell which one, what kind, and how many. Adverbs describe verbs, adjectives, and other adverbs telling where, when, and how. Some adjectives are so similar to their adverb counterparts that they are easily confused. For example:

This is an <u>easy</u> recipe. (adjective describing recipe)

You can make this recipe <u>easily</u>. (adverb describing make)

Most adverbs end in –ly but some do not, such as *never, not, less, almost, more, very, always, well.*

A few adjectives end in –ly, such as *lovely, friendly, chilly, orderly, ugly,* and *likely.*

Even more confusing are flat adverbs that can be used as adverbs or adjectives. They include: *fast, slow, quick, hard, far, close, fine, straight,* and *deep.* Some flat adverbs like *slow* have an *–ly* form. But both adverb forms are correct, despite arguments to the contrary.

Drive slow. (correct)

Drive slowly. (correct)

Good and well are commonly confused. *Good* is always an adjective; *well* is usually an adverb but it can function as an *adjective.*

I am doing good at this. (incorrect)

I am doing well at this. (correct)

Am and *feel* are both linking verbs connecting adjectives to the subject *I* in these examples. When used with these linking verbs, *well* generally refers to physical health.

I am good. (correct)

I am well. (correct)

I do not feel good. (correct)

I do not feel well. (correct)

Bad and badly are also frequently confused. *Bad* is an adjective, so is used with the linking verb *feel. Badly* is an adverb usually used to describe an action.

I feel bad. (correct)

I feel badly. (incorrect)

I played bad. (incorrect)

I played badly. (correct)

Real and really are often confused. *Real* is an adjective meaning authentic; *really* is an adverb meaning actually or very. *Real* is used as an adverb in casual conversation, but should not be used as an adverb in writing.

> *I am real excited. (incorrect)*
> *I really can't go. (correct)*

"Did I do good?" Cook asked, poking her head out of the kitchen.

The queen grimaced but nodded enthusiastically. The rest of the family agreed that the brisket was delicious.

"You roasted it slow and it showed," the king said, smiling.

After she left, the king admitted that he wasn't a fan of flat adverbs. "But we now have a more seriously problem. Er, you know what I mean. I'd like you three to write a mission on adjective-adverb confusion. Then go to planet Sentence and get these parts of speech to return to their homes."

The children agreed and got to work right away.

What does *impudent* mean?

What part of speech is the word *bad*?

Why was the dentist using improper grammar?

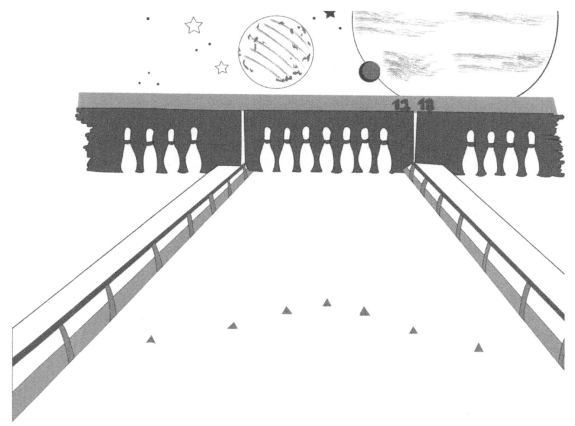

Chapter 25

The queen was excited that she had finally talked her husband into bowling with the family. The queen was a bowler when she was younger and she was eager to see if she had **retained** her skill.

The king had grumbled but had finally **succumbed** to the queen's **entreating**.

The queen asked that bumpers be used on their lane so no one would be throwing balls into the gutters. The king didn't think that would be necessary, but he could see where it would benefit the kids.

★ ★ ★ ★ ★ ★ ★ ★ ★ ★

retained – *kept*

succumbed – *surrendered*

entreating – *pleading*

★ ★ ★ ★ ★ ★ ★ ★ ★ ★

After the royal family set up their lane's scoring machine, the king bowled first. His ball bounced off the left bumper, then the right bumper, taking out just two pins on the far right.

"Don't need the bumpers, huh?" the queen teased.

The king's second roll hit the same spot, so he ended with just two pins down.

The queen was relaxed but confident for her first roll. It was a strike! She was ecstatic and the kids congratulated her.

"It's a game of luck," the king grumbled. When the queen shot him a look, he covered by telling her he was happy for her luck.

"It's skill, not luck," she objected goodnaturedly. "If it's luck, you'll be rolling as many strikes as I do."

The king smiled halfheartedly and encouraged Kirk to roll a strike. Kirk's ball hit the right bumper and bounced to the center of the lane. It struck the pins at an angle, leaving just one standing.

"Kirk almost got a strike!" the king declared.

"That's right. Kirk can get a spare if he takes out the 6 pin. Kirk, move left six boards and then roll," the queen said, positioning him on the lane.

Kirk carefully rolled the ball toward the standing pin. The ball just clipped the pin, causing it to wobble and slowly fall.

"Kirk got a spare!" the king said, patting him on the back in congratulations.

"If Kirk got a spare, Ellen will get a strike," Ellen said.

The king and queen laughed at their daughter's competitiveness.

As Ellen went to release the ball, it slipped, sending it bouncing back and forth between the bumpers. Just three pins were knocked down.

"Ellen can still get a spare," the queen said reassuringly.

"Ellen can still get a spare," Ellen repeated as she aimed the ball carefully. But again, the ball slipped off her fingers, bounced between the bumpers, and ended in the hole she'd created with her first roll.

"Ellen thinks the ball is causing the problem," Ellen said.

Luke frowned. "Ellen is talking funny," he said, as he prepared to roll his first ball. What the roll lacked in power, it made up for in placement. All the pins fell and Luke had a strike.

"Luke has a strike!" the king declared.

"Luke has a strike!" Luke repeated.

The family congratulated him and Luke high-fived Kirk.

113

"Ellen needs a new ball," Ellen said, looking for a different ball in the racks.

"The king rolls next," the queen said.

"Indeed!" the king agreed. The queen laughed.

The king's roll again bounced between the bumpers, hitting just a couple of pins on the right.

"The king will get a spare," the king said after his initial frustration.

"The king is confident," the queen teased.

"The king is very confident," he agreed.

But the king's second ball landed in the gap created by the first. "The king isn't having good luck tonight," he joked.

"The king is correct," the queen said, laughing.

The queen stood up to roll. "The queen will get a second strike," she said confidently.

But her attention was diverted by Ellen who walked up to her and announced, "Ellen can't find another good ball."

"Ellen, Ellen distracted me. The queen can't roll another strike if Ellen interrupts the queen," the queen said. Then she gasped. "Why is the queen talking this way?" she wondered aloud.

"The queen keeps repeating 'Ellen' and 'the queen,'" the king said, agreeing that something wasn't right.

"Bowling is like when Kirk, Luke, Ellen, Mother, and Father were playing a card game and Kirk, Luke, Ellen, Mother, and Father couldn't use—. What are those nouns called again?" Luke asked.

"Pronouns," the king and queen said in unison.

"Yes! Pronouns are the part of speech that prevents repetition of nouns," Kirk said.

"The king is afraid we will have to end our game until we can correct this problem," the king said.

"The king is just trying to avoid losing," the queen teased.

The royal family returned to the castle where the king wasted no time in determining why the pronouns weren't usable.

Screen reported, "Pronouns on planet Sentence have secured an agent to negotiate a new contract with their antecedents. The words say they are pros and should be treated as such."

"That's preposterous," the king stated, his voice rising. "The prefix *pro* doesn't stand for professional in the word *pronoun*. *Pro* in *pronoun* means substitution."

"Dear, don't let the Gremlin make the king angry," the queen said.

"The queen is right. The king is sure the Gremlin arranged for the agent," the king said.

"Kirk has an idea," Kirk said. "What if the guardians ask to serve as the pronouns' agent? Then Kirk, Luke, and Ellen can send a mission asking the guardians to reconnect the pronouns to their antecedents."

"What are antecedents again?" Luke asked.

The king called for *The Guide to Grammar Galaxy*. When it arrived, he explained that pronouns already have a contract with antecedents. He read the article on pronoun-antecedent agreement aloud.

Pronoun-Antecedent Agreement

A **pronoun** takes the place of a noun so sentences aren't repetitive. Personal pronouns refer to people or things and include *I, you, he, she, it, we, they, me, him, her, us,* and *them*. Note that the pronoun *I* is always capitalized.

A noun that comes before and is replaced by a pronoun is called an **antecedent**. *Ante* means before. For example, <u>The captain encouraged his crew.</u> The possessive pronoun *his* refers to the antecedent *captain*. Pronouns and antecedents must agree or match in number and gender.

<u>Singular or Plural Agreement.</u> A singular pronoun must have a singular antecedent. The pronouns *I, me, my, he, him, his, she, her, hers, it,* and *its* are singular. The nouns these pronouns replace must also be singular or one in number.

The pronouns *we, our, ours, they, them, their,* and *theirs* are plural and should replace plural nouns or those that number more than one.

A prepositional phrase or clause after the noun does not determine the number of the pronoun. For example, <u>The box of lasers was placed on its shelf.</u> *Lasers* in the prepositional phrase *of lasers* is plural, but *box* is singular, requiring the singular pronoun *its*.

Compound subjects joined by *and* always take a plural pronoun. For example, <u>All moons and our moon orbit their planets.</u> Even though *moon* is singular, the plural possessive pronoun *their* is used because it is a compound subject.

Compound subjects joined by *or/nor* use a singular or plural pronoun depending

on whether the noun closest to the pronoun is singular or plural. For example, <u>Our planet or other planets follow their orbit around the sun.</u> *Planets* is closest, so the plural possessive pronoun *their* is used. <u>Neither the dogs nor the cat will eat its lunch.</u> *Cat* is closest, so the singular possessive pronoun *its* is used.

Titles or single subjects take a singular pronoun. <u>*Number the Stars* has its fans.</u> <u>Mumps is making its way through college campuses.</u>

<u>Gender Agreement</u>. Male nouns should use *he*, *him*, or *his*. Female nouns should use *she*, *her*, or *hers*. Gender-neutral nouns should use *it*, *its,* or plural pronouns.

When human gender is either or unknown, writers may use both male and female pronouns with the conjunction *or*. <u>A student should have his or her book for class.</u>

Using a plural noun makes for a simpler sentence, however. <u>Students should have their books for class.</u>

Using *they* **or** *their* **with a singular, unknown gender antecedent has also become acceptable in modern usage.** <u>Your sibling may want to have their own room.</u>

Luke sighed. "Being an agent for pronouns will be hard work. No wonder agents get paid a lot!" Luke said.

The king chuckled. "Luke won't be making a lot of money but will be doing this galaxy a tremendous service. Kirk, send a letter to the pronouns about representing them right away. Luke and Ellen, work on a mission called Pronoun-Antecedent Agreement so the mission is ready when Kirk gets approval."

The English children agreed and got to work.

What does *succumbed* mean?

Which type of pronoun do compound subjects take?

Why were pronouns unusable during the family's bowling game?

Chapter 26

The queen received a message from one of her friends imploring her to watch a documentary. "It's about preventing violence," her friend said.

The queen groaned. She wasn't in the mood to watch anything negative but her friend messaged, "You have to watch it." The queen knew this particular friend wouldn't stop **pestering** her until she relented.

★ ★ ★ ★ ★ ★ ★ ★ ★ ★

pestering – *bothering*

forlorn – *sad*

anarchy – *chaos*

★ ★ ★ ★ ★ ★ ★ ★ ★ ★

She took her tablet to the kitchen to get a cup of tea and a cookie, hoping the snack would make the documentary more enjoyable. When Cook asked what she was up to, the queen suggested she watch with her.

"Is it one of those depressing videos?" Cook asked, hesitating.

"Probably," the queen said, laughing. "Will you watch it with me?"

Cook agreed and poured herself a cup of tea.

Ominous music played while images of **forlorn** and angry people filled the screen. The narrator repeated statistics about violence in the galaxy being on the rise.

"The answer to this epidemic of violence is unexpected," the narrator said.

The video switched to an interview with Professor **Anarchy**. "In our research, we discovered something unexpected," the professor said. "The root of violence, we've learned, is possessiveness—claiming ownership and then wanting more. If we eliminate possessiveness, violence decreases dramatically.

"Traditional wisdom is that possessiveness is a character trait that is difficult to change. But we know that language has a direct effect on character. Change the language and you change character. Other galaxies have had great success in limiting possessive nouns and pronouns specifically. I almost hate to repeat them because of the threat of violence, but pronouns like *mine*, *our*, and *hers* are dangerous. Possessive nouns like *king's*, *galaxy's*, and *Ellen's* are also a threat."

Cook and the queen gasped simultaneously.

"So, what are you saying, Professor?" the interviewer asked.

"I'm saying that a peaceful galaxy requires a ban of possessive nouns and pronouns," he said emphatically.

The screen changed to a web address. "If you want to end violence in the galaxy, go to EndPossessiveness.com and sign the petition. Together we can achieve peace," the narrator said.

Another message from the queen's friend appeared on the tablet. "Did you watch it?" she asked.

"Yes," the queen typed.

"Are you going to get your husband to take action?" came the reply.

"What do I say?" the queen asked Cook, as she repeated her friend's message.

"When I don't know what to say, I just ignore the message," Cook said.

"I'll remember that," the queen said, laughing. "I need to talk to the king about this," she added.

"Are you sure you have to? Isn't this your friend who sends you all the crazy videos?" When the queen nodded, Cook said, "I don't think it's anything worth worrying about. Why put the king in a bad mood?"

The queen smiled appreciatively. "You're right. I'm so glad you're my friend," she said, squeezing Cook's hand.

That evening, the king was late for dinner and he was irate.

"What's wrong, dear?" the queen asked. "Cook has made one of your favorite dishes," she said to encourage him.

"What's wrong is that my favorite dish may not be mine at all!" he shouted.

The queen encouraged him to lower his volume. "What do you mean?"

"A video about violence with a million views has people demanding a ban on possessive nouns and pronouns," the king explained in a quieter voice.

"Did you say a million views?" the queen asked.

"Yes, and I don't know why. It's not even a great video," the king said.

"I agree," the queen added.

The king was shocked. "You've seen it? Why didn't you tell me?" he asked.

"I didn't think it would have any effect," the queen answered apologetically.

Cook entered the dining room. "It's my fault, Your Highness. The queen wanted to tell you. I didn't think it was necessary. I thought it would spoil your dinner. I'm sorry."

The king pardoned them both immediately.

"Can we help?" Kirk asked.

The king thought for a moment. "Yes, I believe you can. People don't understand how important possessive nouns and pronouns are. Language is powerful but these words don't make people possessive and they certainly don't make them violent. Could you craft a mission to teach the guardians that?" he asked.

The three English children agreed to get started after dinner. They reviewed information on possessive nouns and pronouns from *The Guide to Grammar Galaxy* and created a mission by the same name.

Possessive Nouns and Pronouns
Possessive nouns and pronouns show ownership. **Possessive nouns are created by adding an apostrophe + an s ('s) to the end of the noun.** the throne belonging to the king = king's throne the bone belonging to Comet = Comet's bone **The exception to this rule is for plural nouns (showing more than one) that already end in s. In this case, only the apostrophe is added to the end of the word.** the leader belonging to the aliens – aliens' leader the galaxy belonging to the stars = the stars' galaxy The apostrophe goes after the owner or owners. *The childrens' books* is incorrect because the books don't belong to the childrens. Ask who the item belongs to and add the apostrophe to that. Include an **s** if the owner is singular. *The princess's shoe* is correct. There is only one princess and the shoe belongs to her. Princess is

singular, so 's is added. *The princesses' shoes* is also correct. The shoes belong to the princesses. Princesses is plural and ends in s. Only an apostrophe is added.

Possessive pronouns include its, my, mine, your, yours, his, her, hers, our, ours, their, theirs, and whose. <u>Possessive pronouns do not have apostrophes.</u> *It's* is a contraction for *it is* and *who's* is a contraction for *who is*. They are not possessive pronouns.

What does *forlorn* mean?

Do possessive pronouns include apostrophes?

Why should viewers be suspicious of the professor's opinion on possessive nouns and pronouns?

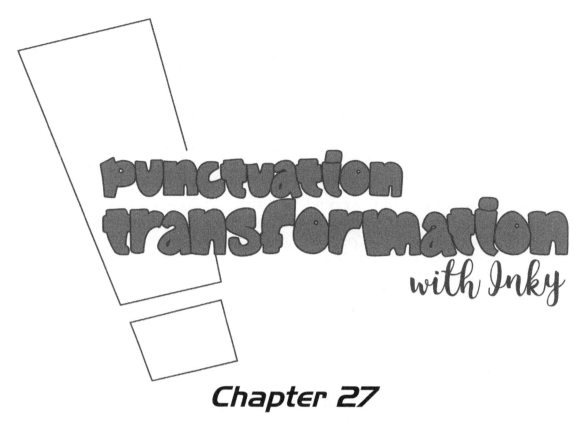

Chapter 27

The royal family was watching a show in the media room when a commercial for a new program began.

"You loved her in Contraction Nation. Now Inky is back in an all-new show the critics are raving about—*Punctuation Transformation*," the announcer said.

Inky appeared on screen, adding punctuation to a sentence. "Sentences want what we all want—to matter," she said. "I just help them be more of who they are."

"That's beautiful," the queen said, sniffling.

"It's emotional **twaddle**," the king said, disagreeing. "Every time that girl gets a new show, there's a crisis."

"She's so passionate about what she does. And it's clear she's **evolving**. I bet there will be no problems this time," the queen said.

★ ★ ★ ★ ★ ★ ★ ★ ★ ★

twaddle – nonsense
evolving – changing
starry-eyed – dreamy

★ ★ ★ ★ ★ ★ ★ ★ ★ ★

The king rolled his eyes.

"I love her," Ellen said with a **starry-eyed** look.

The king was tempted to make a sarcastic retort, but he knew it was no use.

The next week, the family gathered to watch *Punctuation Transformation*. The queen had asked Cook to make popcorn, so the king would be too busy eating to critique the show. Her plan was working as the program started.

The first sentence that worked with Inky was *I need help*. A narrator explained that the sentence had been left without an end mark. The sentence had reportedly told the show's producers that it felt like something was missing.

"*It* told them that," the king said in disbelief.

"Dear, please don't talk while you're eating," the queen said, hoping to get him out of critique mode.

Inky looked over the sentence carefully, nodding. Then she went to work. She added quotation marks around the word *help*. "*Help* is this sentence's truth. That's what I really want to bring attention to," she said.

The king jumped up, spilling his bowl of popcorn on the floor. "You don't bring attention to a word by putting it in quotes!" he yelled.

"Dear, calm down," the queen urged.

"I won't just sit quietly by and watch them destroy this galaxy," he said angrily.

"Don't you think that's a little hyperbolic?" the queen asked.

The king thought better of his angry retort and asked Screen to pause the show. Then he requested that *The Guide to Grammar Galaxy* be brought to the media room.

"We will not watch any more of this until we review guidelines for using punctuation," he said.

When the book arrived, he read them entries on commas, end marks, and quotation marks.

Commas
A comma is a punctuation mark (,) that is used to show a pause between sentence parts. Proper usage can prevent confusion. There are several rules for the correct use of commas.

First, commas are used to separate words in a list of three or more items. The children love reading, writing, and playing games.

The use of a comma before the word *and* at the end of a list is known as the Oxford comma. If you use it in your writing, you should use it consistently.

A second rule for comma usage is to separate the name of the person you are speaking to with commas. Note the difference in meanings below:

I will call you, Angel. (The person is going to call someone who is named Angel.)

I will call you Angel. (The person is giving someone the name Angel.)

A third rule for comma usage is to separate two or more coordinate adjectives with commas. Coordinate adjectives make sense when written in reverse order or when written with *and* between them. Colors and numbers are non-coordinate adjectives that do not require commas.

My little sister loves the song "Three Blind Mice." (non-coordinate)

She also loves the big, famous mouse named Mickey. (coordinate)

End Marks

There are three end marks: the period, question mark, and exclamation point. All three punctuation marks indicate the end of a sentence. Periods are used at the end of statements or **declarative** sentences. Sentences that declare something usually end in periods. Question marks are at the end of questions. *Interrogate* means to question, so these sentences are called **interrogative** sentences. They often begin with *who, what, where, when, why,* and *how*. Finally, exclamation marks come at the end of sentences that express strong emotion. These are called **exclamatory** sentences.

Quotation Marks

Quotation marks (") are punctuation usually used to show the exact words that someone said. They indicate a **direct quote**.

He said, "We don't know anything about it."

A comma or end mark comes before a quote and the first word of a quote is capitalized. A comma or end mark also goes *inside* the last set of quotation marks.

"We don't know anything about it," he said.

Quotation marks are not used for a summary of what someone said.

He said they didn't know anything about it.

This type of report is called an **indirect quote**.

If the person being quoted repeats a quote by someone else, use single quotation marks (') around the secondary quote.

An aerospace engineer said, "My favorite quote from astronaut Sally Ride is 'The stars don't look bigger, but they do look brighter.'"

Quotation marks may also be used to express doubt, so they should not be used for emphasis. Use bold or italic type instead.

She says she is a "model," but she just shares outfits on social media.
(correct expression of doubt)

The bakery's sign advertises "fresh" bread.
(incorrect expression of emphasis that encourages doubt)

"Inky sure has to know a lot about punctuation to do her job," Luke said.

"Yes, and it's clear to me that she doesn't know these rules," the king said.

"I have an idea!" Ellen said enthusiastically. "We can ask Inky to join us as a Guardian of the Galaxy."

"Hm," the king began. "I'm not sure about that. She's an adult and a television star."

"Dear, I think it's a splendid idea if she would agree to it. We'll have even more guardians joining us," the queen said.

"You make a good point. All right. I'll allow it. Create a mission on these punctuation marks and take it to her. If she agrees to read and follow the rules, she's in," the king said.

"Thank you!" Ellen gushed, hugging him.

The three official guardians got to work on a mission that would help Inky and would remind current guardians how to use commas, end marks, and quotation marks correctly.

What does *twaddle* mean?

When should you use a single quotation mark?

Which rule did Inky break in punctuating the sentence I need help?

Unit V: Adventures in Composition & Speaking

Chapter 28

Kirk was in the computer lab, writing an article for a new robotics journal. The king had **advocated** it as a good way to reach an expanded audience.

★ ★ ★ ★ ★ ★ ★ ★ ★ ★

advocated – *encouraged*
wholeheartedly – *enthusiastically*

★ ★ ★ ★ ★ ★ ★ ★ ★ ★

But Kirk was growing more and more frustrated as he worked. He knew what he wanted to say, but his computer's response time was considerably slowed.

He checked the year the computer was manufactured and was surprised that it had been built when Luke was a baby. No wonder it was slow!

He left his work and found his father in his study. He told him of the difficulty he'd had and what he'd discovered. "May we get an updated computer? I need a faster operating system and a computer that will run the latest robotics software," Kirk explained.

The king smiled. "I bet I'm going to surprise you by saying yes. I know how important it is to your work to have an updated system," he said.

Kirk smiled in return and thanked his father **wholeheartedly**.

As they were talking, Ellen joined them. "Father, look at this," she said. "I'm writing on this tablet and something's wrong. Look how slow it is," she said, demonstrating. "This assignment is due tomorrow. How am I supposed to write on a tablet that lags like this?"

The king glanced at Kirk who gave him a sympathetic smile.

"Are you asking for a new tablet?" the king asked.

"Yes, but I know you don't want to spend the money—" she began in a rush.

"Yes," the king said.

"Yes, what?" Ellen asked.

"Yes, I will order a new tablet."

"You will?" Ellen was astonished and hugged him, thanking him profusely.

"Well, Kirk has pointed out that our devices are outdated. I know you use them to protect the galaxy," the king said. He was enjoying having his children's **favor**.

★ ★ ★ ★ ★ ★ ★ ★ ★ ★

favor – *approval*

★ ★ ★ ★ ★ ★ ★ ★ ★ ★

A week later, Kirk and Ellen were delighted to see that their new devices had been delivered. They both got busy setting them up.

At dinner that evening, the king asked how the new computer and tablet were working. He was surprised to get glum reactions from both Kirk and Ellen.

"What's wrong? We ordered the correct devices, did we not?" the king asked.

"Yes, yes, we did," Ellen said quickly. Kirk nodded to agree.

"Then what's wrong?" the king asked.

"Unfortunately, the new computer is still quite slow," Kirk said, hoping his father wouldn't be angry.

"Yes, my new tablet is slow, too," Ellen agreed.

Before the king could voice his displeasure, Kirk said, "That's it!"

"What's it?" the queen asked.

"It has to be our network. I thought it was our outdated devices," Kirk explained.

When he saw his father reddening, Kirk said, "We still needed new devices. But we also need to update the network to improve the speed."

"More money," the king grumbled.

"Dear, remember how proud you are of the children. You said you wanted to give them everything they need to learn and protect this galaxy," the queen said.

"I said that, did I?" the king joked. The children smiled. "All right," the king said. "I will have our programmer update our system. I'm a little surprised he didn't take initiative on that," he said.

The next day, the head programmer announced to the king that their system was updated. He had also taken steps to increase their network speed.

"Excellent!" the king said approvingly. He called Kirk and Ellen to his study and gave them the good news.

But later that day, both children remained frustrated. Their devices were running too slowly to write with. They didn't want to tell their father, but he found them and asked if the update had solved the problem.

The king was very unhappy when he heard of the continuing slow speed. That's when Kirk had another thought. "You don't think the Gremlin could be behind it, do you?" he asked his father.

The king sighed. "Why didn't I think of that? Screen, give me a status report on the galaxy, please," he said.

"Your Majesty, all is well. The speed drills you ordered on planet Spelling are being held daily," Screen replied.

"What speed drills?" the king asked. "Never mind. Give me video footage of the drills, will you?"

Video of letters running to take their place in words appeared on the screen. As the king, Kirk, and Ellen watched, they could see the letters were exhausted. They started out running, but ended up walking, and even fainting.

"This must be why our writing is so slow," Kirk said.

"I'm surprised Luke hasn't been complaining," the king said.

"He always thinks writing takes forever," Ellen joked.

"What are you going to do?" Kirk asked.

"First, I'm going to call off these speed drills on planet Sentence. Then I'm going to start them here on planet English," the king said.

"What do you mean?" Ellen asked.

"When you mentioned Luke and writing speed, you reminded me how important is to keep our writing and typing speed up. I would like you three to send out a mission that will help the guardians increase their handwriting and typing speed. Be sure to include dictation exercises."

"Why dictation?" Kirk asked.

"Because it increases writing speed while it teaches spelling and grammar," the king explained.

Kirk and Ellen agreed. They found Luke and began working on a mission they called Handwriting, Keyboarding, and Dictation.

What does *favor* mean?

What does dictation teach?

Why was the children's writing so slow?

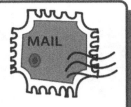

MAIL

FISHY TECH

Kirk, Luke, & Ellen
1 Castle Way
Planet English 12345

Chapter 29

"The guardians have mail!" the king announced cheerfully.

"Great!" Ellen responded, tearing the envelope her father handed her.

"What is it?" Luke asked eagerly.

"I don't know. Let me read it," Ellen replied.

The family remained quiet while Ellen read. "It's from a company called **Fishy** Tech," she began.

★ ★ ★ ★ ★ ★ ★ ★ ★ ★

fishy – *suspicious*

★ ★ ★ ★ ★ ★ ★ ★ ★ ★

"Another game to try?" Luke suggested.

"Not quite. This company has developed new dictation software. They want us to try it and give them feedback."

"Boring," Luke said, earning a warning look from his mother.

"What makes it different?" Kirk asked.

"They say it's **distinctive** because it **anticipates** what you're going to say, so it's even faster than normal dictation software," Ellen explained. "It could save us time."

"I like that!" Luke said.

"Should we say yes, Father?" Ellen asked.

"Why not? It will be a good opportunity for you to review your proofreading. I'd like all the guardians to practice using dictation software," the king said.

He led the three children to the castle library where he read articles on dictation software and proofreading from *The Guide to Grammar Galaxy*.

★ ★ ★ ★ ★ ★ ★ ★ ★

distinctive – *unique*

anticipates – *predicts*

★ ★ ★ ★ ★ ★ ★ ★ ★

Dictation Software

Dictation software allows writers to produce text quickly. A good typing speed is 60 words per minute, while words can be spoken at more than twice that rate.

Dictation software is a good tool for producing a first draft, not a final paper. Editing is typically done with a keyboard.

To produce a quality draft:

Practice to improve your speed and accuracy. You'll need to remember to say punctuation marks aloud, for example.

Consider using a headset that eliminates outside noise. Pronounce words clearly.

Learn your software's basic commands. Most software will respond to punctuation names and to "new paragraph," but study the commands that are unique to your program.

Pause between thoughts and speak in complete sentences. Thinking before speaking will eliminate filler words like *uh* and *um*.

Speak the sentence correctly a second time, rather than trying to edit as you speak.

Say "asterisk" to mark places that require more information or editing later. You will search your document for * when using a keyboard.

When proofreading your paper, look carefully for incorrect homophones. Look for the wrong form of it's/its, to/too/two, your/you're and there/their/they're.

Proofreading

Proofreading is carefully checking writing for grammar, spelling, and typing errors (also known as typos).
   Wait some time before editing and proofreading your own work. Reading a paper aloud can help you notice errors. Use a text-to-speech program if you prefer. Having someone else proofread your work is also a good idea.
   You or your proofreader will use marks to show changes that need to be made. Review the most common marks in the following chart.

Mark	Meaning	Mark	Meaning
 ℮	delete	⁋	new paragraph
≡	capitalize	/	make lower case
∧	insert	 ⌄	insert comma
#	add space	 ◡	close gap
⊙	add period	 ∽	transpose (trade places)
~~word~~	replace	sp	spelling error

"How are we going to test the software?" Luke asked.

"You can try dictating something already in print to start," the king said. "Then we can have you and the guardians write an essay about your hobbies. Our interests outside of work make us happier and more interesting people."

The three English children liked that idea. Ellen agreed to contact the company and arrange for access to the software. Then they wrote a mission called Proofreading and Dictation Software for the guardians.

What does *distinctive* mean?

What should you do if you've said a sentence poorly while using dictation software?

Why should the king have been suspicious about the company providing the software?

Chapter 30

The king sat in the sunroom reading on an overcast day. Luke complained of being bored, so the king suggested that he join him in reading.

Luke left to get a book from his bedchamber, returning with Comet as his heels. "We're going to read, boy, and then I'll teach you some tricks," Luke said, petting his dog.

As Luke settled into reading, he couldn't help but chuckle a few times. He was reading a title a librarian had recommended. She'd said that kids his age found it very funny. Luke was glad he'd taken her advice.

The king was a bit distracted when Luke chuckled, but he was glad to see him enjoying his book. He finally asked him what was so funny.

Luke began explaining and the king waved him off. "I don't think you retelling it will be as funny. Why don't you read it to me?" he suggested.

"Okay," Luke said **diffidently**. He began reading slowly in broken phrases. His poor **articulation** and word emphasis **obfuscated** the humor.

★ ★ ★ ★ ★ ★ ★ ★ ★ ★

diffidently – *self-consciously*

articulation – *pronunciation*

obfuscated – *concealed*

★ ★ ★ ★ ★ ★ ★ ★ ★ ★

The king was unhappy with the way Luke was reading. But he remembered his wife telling him to be more aware of his children's feelings. Normally, he would tell Luke he hadn't been reading aloud regularly and his slow reading was the result. This time he decided to take a different approach.

"Luke, I'm concerned about your reading. I think the Gremlin is responsible. I'm going to find out what he's done this time to interfere with reading fluency," he said.

"Okay, Father. I'm sorry the Gremlin never lets you have a day off."

The king laughed. "That's true! One positive thing I can say about him is he's persistent. You and your siblings will likely have a mission to send out when I get to the bottom of this. I'll let you know."

Luke nodded and went to get Comet some training treats.

In his study, the king asked Screen for a status report on planet Composition.

"I have nothing newsworthy to report there, Your Highness," Screen replied.

"All right. How about planet Sentence then?" the king asked.

Screen paused a moment. "No, Your Highness, nothing appears to be amiss. Even the weather is beautiful."

"That's strange. It must be something that hasn't yet made the news," the king wondered aloud.

"Would you like me to give you video footage, Sire?" Screen asked.

"That's brilliant. Yes, thank you."

A video feed of both planets appeared on the Screen. The scene changed several times, but the king didn't notice anything unusual.

"Could the problem be on another planet?" Screen suggested.

"I suppose?" the king said, less than confidently.

After another short pause, Screen reported that nothing newsworthy was occurring on planets Spelling or Vocabulary either.

"That's it!" the king said, elated.

"What's it, Your Highness?"

"The Gremlin is blocking the feed. And He is supplying a phony video feed, making it look like all is well," the king explained.

Without waiting for a response from Screen, the king messaged his three children to come to his study.

When they arrived, he explained his theory. He asked them to travel to planets Composition and Sentence to determine what was really happening. They would have to take the spaceporter.

The children were excited to investigate. They left for planet Composition first. Upon arrival, they didn't notice anything unusual. They walked the peaceful streets and talked to Grammar Patrol to confirm that operations were running smoothly.

Using his communicator, Kirk gave the king the news.

"I'd like you to go to planet Sentence now. That must be the source of the problem," the king said.

The children used their communicators to activate the spaceporter and were immediately on planet Sentence. As with planet Composition, everything seemed to be in order. They walked some neighborhoods and again met with Grammar Patrol.

When Kirk gave their father the positive report, the king was mystified. "Wait! I've got it. Somehow the Gremlin has hypnotized the sentences," the king said.

"What are you talking about?" the queen asked him while he talked with Kirk.

The king explained that Luke was reading aloud slowly and that the children hadn't found an explanation for it on the planets. Therefore, it had to be hypnotism.

"Do you know the saying 'The simplest explanation is the best explanation?'" the queen asked.

"Of course I do. What are you saying?" the king asked, but it was clear he knew exactly what she was saying. "Kirk, let me speak to Luke, please," the king said.

When he was on the call, the king asked, "Luke, have you been reading aloud much lately?"

Luke began stammering.

"I'll take that as a no. Please come home so we can review the importance of reading fluency," the king said.

When the children returned, the king read them the article on reading fluency from *The Guide to Grammar Galaxy*.

Reading Fluency

Reading fluency or smoothness requires knowledge of phonics and vocabulary. Before reading aloud, make sure you know all the words and how they should be pronounced or spoken. Practice, practice, practice to improve speed. With time, you can be saying one word and reading the next few or noticing upcoming punctuation. Reading skills improve by imitating another reader. Reading while listening to an audiobook is another strategy for improving fluency.

Some reading aloud tips include:

1. Clearly pronounce each word, emphasizing or stressing the words that rhyme in poetry.

---

2. When reading in public, look up from the material to make eye contact occasionally. Hold your finger at the place you last read so you won't lose your place.

3. Use different voices for characters in a children's book.

4. Change your loudness or speed every so often to keep listeners' attention.

5. Drop your tone when coming to a period to signal the end of a sentence.

"Sorry I haven't been reading aloud, Father," Luke said.

"I shouldn't have assumed it was the Gremlin's doing," the king said. "But I appreciate you taking responsibility," he said, smiling. "Now I'd like all three of you to send out a mission on reading fluency. I'm sure Luke isn't the only one who hasn't been reading aloud regularly."

What does *diffidently* mean?

What should happen to your tone when coming to the end of a sentence you are reading aloud?

Why did the king think the Gremlin was at fault for Luke's slow reading?

Chapter 31

"I heard you chatting on your communicator. Were you talking to Cher?" the queen asked Ellen one Saturday afternoon.

"No, it was Alexis," she answered.

"Alexis? I haven't heard you talk about her before."

"We've gotten to be friends through Grammar Girls," Ellen explained.

"Well, that's wonderful. Why don't you have her come over to visit sometime?" the queen suggested.

"Sometime," Ellen said in a **noncommittal** way. "She invited me to her house today. May I go?"

"We don't know her family," the queen said **circumspectly**.

"You can meet them when you drop me off," Ellen said **glibly**.

★ ★ ★ ★ ★ ★ ★ ★ ★ ★

noncommittal – *indecisive*

circumspectly – *cautiously*

glibly – *smoothly*

★ ★ ★ ★ ★ ★ ★ ★ ★ ★

"Hm. I suppose that would be okay."

"Thanks, Mother," Ellen said. "We'll go after lunch."

The queen didn't like Ellen's attitude about the visit, but she put it out of her mind.

Alexis's mother met the queen and Ellen at the door. "It's a delight to meet you," her mother said to the queen.

"The pleasure is all mine," the queen said courteously.

Alexis appeared at the door and grabbed Ellen by the hand, drawing her inside.

"Wait!" the queen said urgently. Then she realized she needed to seem casual. "I wanted to meet you, too," she told Alexis.

"Sure," Alexis said, shrugging. "Nice to meet you. You can come back after dinner to get her," she said dismissively.

"Uh, all right. I will see you then, dear," she told Ellen.

"I'm sure they will have fun," Alexis's mother said pleasantly.

The queen nodded as loud music began playing from inside the house. "Why don't I give you my communicator number," the queen suggested anxiously. "You can reach me if there are any problems."

"They'll be fine," Alexis's mother said, smiling to reassure the queen.

"You're probably thinking I'm one of those spacecopter moms," the queen said, laughing at herself.

Alexis's mother just smiled and said she would see her after dinner sometime.

The queen counted the hours until it was time for her to pick up Ellen. She didn't know why she was so uneasy, but she was thrilled when Ellen came to the door. The queen thanked Alexis's mother for hosting her. Alexis was not at the door to say goodbye.

On the way home, the queen asked Ellen about the visit.

"After you left," Ellen said.

"Yes, after I left?" the queen asked.

"Even though you were nervous about the visit," Ellen said.

"Yes, I was nervous about the visit. I'm sorry. It's hard when your daughter is growing up," the queen said apologetically.

"Now that you've met her."

"Yes, I've met her."

"Because she's not like Cher," Ellen said.

"I can see that."

"If you don't approve."

"I didn't say I don't approve," the queen said, confused by Ellen's attitude.

"In case you don't want me to visit again."

"I didn't say that, either," the queen said. "Why don't you just tell me what you did this afternoon?" She hoped to get Ellen focusing on the positive.

"After you left, although I know you don't approve, as soon as we started listening to music, before I knew it, by the time dinner was ready, in case you are worried, now that we're on our way home, since you've met her and her mother, whenever we get together again, whether or not you like her," Ellen said without taking a breath.

The queen's eyes grew wide. She wondered what to say and decided to side hug her daughter instead. "I'm glad you had a good time," she added.

After they arrived home and Ellen was in her bedchamber, the queen expressed her concerns to the king. "I don't even know this girl!" the queen said. "But I do know that Ellen is acting very strangely after spending time with her. I don't like this friendship."

"Strangely how?" the king asked.

"Well, she doesn't finish her sentences for one. And the next moment she is going on and on about her visit but not really saying anything."

"And you think this is abnormal?" the king joked.

"I'm being serious! This isn't like her," the queen objected.

"Dear, let's get some rest. I have a feeling she will be back to normal tomorrow. Ellen's new independence is hard for you to accept. I understand that."

"I don't think that's it. But I am tired," the queen said.

When she awoke the next morning, the queen concluded that she had overreacted to Ellen's behavior. She was sure she had been the same with her girlfriends at that age. She looked forward to seeing Ellen at breakfast and being reassured that all was well.

But Ellen's attitude seemed much the same. "Supposing I want to go to Alexis's house next weekend," she said.

140

"Again?" Luke asked.

Both the queen and Ellen hushed him.

"Provided that her mother is there to supervise us," Ellen said.

"And?" the queen prodded her.

"And? Since I rarely spend time with friends, unless you can give me a good reason not to go, whether or not it's here or at her house, while Kirk spends time with his robotics team, by the time I'm an adult, because I like Alexis, as much as possible. Okay?" she said in a rush.

It was the king's turn to be wide-eyed. Because he was afraid of saying the wrong thing, he called out to Cook for another serving of eggs.

The queen was despairing that she had lost her daughter to a friend who was a poor influence when Luke chimed in.

"Till I'm your age, supposing I want to go to a friend's house, only if I have their approval, because we're royals, now that you've set an example, in the event that I get an invitation, even though there have been some problems, by the time I'm your age, as long as I'm caught up with work," Luke said, breathless when he was finished.

"So it's not just Ellen," the queen said looking to her husband.

"As much as I wish it weren't so," the king said, sighing. "Screen, give me video footage of new arrivals to planet Sentence," he ordered.

The king watched for a few minutes and announced, "As I expected." He requested that *The Guide to Grammar Galaxy* be brought to him. When it arrived, he read articles on what qualifies as a correct sentence.

Sentences and Sentence Fragments

You can remember the rules for a sentence with this rhyme:

A sentence starts with a capital letter, my friend,
And has a period, exclamation, or question mark at the end.
A sentence needs a subject, the who or what it's about.
It also needs a verb like *is*, *go*, *sing*, or *shout*.
Instead of a sentence, it's a fragment you've got
if all the words together are not a complete thought.

A sentence fragment may begin with a capital letter and have an end mark but is missing a subject, verb, or a complete thought. For example,

The star exploded. (complete sentence)

After the star exploded. (sentence fragment, not a complete thought)

And exploded in a huge fireball. (sentence fragment, no subject, not a complete thought)

The exploding star. (sentence fragment, no verb, not a complete thought)

Dependent and Independent Clauses

A dependent clause (also called a subordinate clause) requires an independent clause to make sense. An independent clause can stand alone as a complete sentence.

After we had dinner (dependent clause)
we went to a movie (independent clause)

When a subordinating conjunction joins dependent and independent clauses, a complex sentence is formed. Dependent clauses with a subordinating conjunction at the beginning of a sentence are normally followed by a comma.

After we had dinner, we went to a movie. (complex sentence)

See the chart with common subordinating conjunctions below.

Common Subordinating Conjunctions		
after	in order (that)	when
although	now that	whenever
as	once	where
as soon as	since	wherever
because	so that	whether
before	than	while
even if	that	why
even though	though	
how	till	

if	unless	
in case	until	

Run-On Sentences

A run-on sentence is an incorrect grammatical structure in which two or more independent clauses are joined without one of the following: a period, semicolon (;), or comma and coordinating conjunction. Run-on sentences are difficult to read and confusing. Correct them by identifying the independent clauses (i.e. subject and predicate combinations). Then add a period, semicolon, or coordinating conjunction with a comma. A sentence following a newly added period must begin with a capital letter.

Birds migrate north and south they are usually seeking a better food supply. *(run-on)*

Birds migrate north and south. They are usually seeking a better food supply. *(corrected with a period and a capitalized They)*

A comma splice is one form of run-on sentence. A comma, rather than a period or semicolon, is used between independent clauses. To find many comma splices, look for a comma followed by the pronouns *he, she, it, we,* or *they.*

Birds migrate north and south, they are usually seeking a better food supply. *(incorrect comma splice)*

A semicolon may be used to join closely related sentences. The independent clause after the semicolon is not capitalized.

Birds migrate north and south; they are usually seeking a better food supply.

A comma, followed by a coordinating conjunction (for, and, nor, but, or, yet, so) can also be used to correct a run-on sentence.

Birds migrate north and south, and they are usually seeking a better food supply.

Grammatically correct sentences are also considered run-ons if too many independent clauses are connected.

Birds migrate north and south, and they migrate long distances, and they are usually seeking a better food supply, but some birds migrate for more daylight, and the daylight gives birds more time for mating. *(run-on with too many coordinating conjunctions)*

"Sentence fragments are once again being accepted on planet Sentence," the king said. "They seem to be joining together to form run-on sentences. I need you to send out a mission on sentences. But

I also need you to go to planet Sentence and make sure fragments aren't being allowed entry."

The three English children agreed and got to work immediately after breakfast.

What does *circumspectly* mean?

What five things are required for a complete sentence?

Why was the queen concerned about Ellen's new friendship with Alexis?

Chapter 32

The king began grumbling while reading the paper one morning.

"I don't know why you start your day with bad news," the queen said, chiding him.

"I don't know, either," the king said.

"What is it this time?" the queen asked.

"A new study suggests that while our young people are getting good scores on multiple-choice tests, they don't really know the material. They asked young people some simple questions about grammar that they couldn't answer."

"You mean, they are memorizing for the test and then forgetting it?" the queen asked.

"Precisely."

"That's the problem with tests, though. There is no way to fix it," the queen stated.

"Lots of practice and review should help," the king replied.

"Yes, it should. Now have some tea," the queen said playfully.

After breakfast, the king received a call from the prime minister. "Your Majesty, I trust you read the piece in today's paper about testing," he said.

The king wanted to remember to tell the queen that this was one reason to read the paper daily. "I did indeed," he answered.

"Good. Members of Parliament did as well. They are ready to do something about it."

"What do you mean?" the king asked, suddenly alarmed.

"They have **floated dismantling** the guardian program for one," he said.

"You can't be serious!" the king cried.

★ ★ ★ ★ ★ ★ ★ ★ ★

floated – *proposed*

dismantling – *undoing*

★ ★ ★ ★ ★ ★ ★ ★ ★

"I'm afraid I am. Some members have come to me and said that if our young people aren't really learning, we may as well shift our focus."

"To what?" the king said, still shaken by the suggestion of discontinuing the guardian program.

"New textbooks."

"I can't believe this. How will textbooks help?" the king asked.

"The argument is that you and I remember our grammar, right? We learned with textbooks," the prime minister explained.

"I won't let this happen without a fight," the king said.

"I expected as much," the prime minister said, smiling.

The king went for a walk in the garden, hoping to have some insight into this latest problem. "Multiple-choice tests aren't a good indicator of what our young people know. Could we do away with tests?" he asked aloud. He shook his head. "They would never agree to that. What if we used a different test format, one that truly demonstrates a student's knowledge? That's it!" he said with enthusiasm.

Comet found him then, and the king began playing fetch with him.

When he and Comet returned to the castle, he had the kids join him in their library. He explained that the disconnect between test scores and knowledge had Parliament considering an end to the guardian program.

"They wouldn't do that, would they?" Luke asked.

The king's expression changed to a quizzical one. "Why *would* they do that?" he asked himself. "All this time I've assumed this was Parliament's idea. I should have known that the Gremlin has someone lobbying against the guardians. This has nothing to do with testing!" he said, feeling **liberated**.

★ ★ ★ ★ ★ ★ ★ ★ ★ ★

liberated – *freed*

★ ★ ★ ★ ★ ★ ★ ★ ★ ★

"Now what do we do?" Kirk asked.

"We move forward with my idea. There is another type of test that is a better indicator of what students know called the essay exam. An essay exam requires written, paragraph answers. I'll read you what *The Guide to Grammar Galaxy* has to say."

Paragraphs

A paragraph is a part of a written composition about one topic. It may also be the dialogue of one speaker. A paragraph is made up of one or more sentences.

Paragraphs begin on a new line. The first line of a paragraph is usually indented, beginning a few spaces to the right of the margin. The white space around paragraphs makes papers and books easier to read. A new paragraph in fiction can make it clear that another character is speaking.

A good nonfiction paragraph includes a topic sentence, supporting sentences, and a concluding sentence. The topic sentence is usually the first sentence. It explains what the rest of the paragraph will be about. Supporting sentences give more information about the topic. A concluding sentence usually summarizes what has been said. It can also tell what happened.

Essay Exams

An essay exam requires answers written in paragraph form. Use these five guidelines for writing a quality essay-exam response:

First, write a brief outline of your answer, including your thesis statement (topic sentence) and supporting points in logical order. It is customary to have three main points.

Second, write the introductory sentence(s), leaving a space between lines for editing. Use keywords from the question in stating your thesis and preview your main points.

Third, write your main points with examples or supporting evidence. In longer essays, each main point will be a separate paragraph. Use transition words between main points (e.g., second, in addition, a final example).

Fourth, write your concluding sentence(s). Summarize what you've written, using a keyword from the question.

Finally, use the remaining time to edit your work. Check your spelling and grammar, and make sure your main points support your thesis statement.

If you follow these guidelines, you will write excellent responses to essay exams.

(Note that this article could be considered an essay answer to the question "What is an essay exam?")

"You want us to send out a mission on essay exams, right?" Ellen asked.

"I do indeed," the king said smiling. "I want our guardians to demonstrate what they know. Then I will personally lobby Parliament to forget about ending the guardian program."

The three English children worked with their father to create a mission.

What does *floated* mean in the story?

What is the topic sentence of an essay exam response called?

What does the king think is behind Parliament's idea of dismantling the guardian program?

Chapter 33

The king and queen were walking to breakfast when the queen asked him, "Aren't you speaking for the Periodical Association this evening?"

The king croaked out an affirmation and grasped his throat in alarm.

"You just need some hot tea," the queen reassured him.

The king nodded, hoping she was right.

But at breakfast, the king's laryngitis was confirmed. He couldn't speak above a whisper.

"Such a shame that you'll have to cancel," the queen said.

The king shook his head no.

"You can't be thinking of speaking with your voice like that?" she asked.

The king shook his head again.

"What then?" the queen asked.

The king gestured to Kirk.

"Me?" Kirk asked in shock. "You want me to speak in your place?"

The king nodded and smiled.

"Isn't this an after-dinner speech, though? Kirk hasn't ever given that kind of speech," the queen said.

"What's an after-dinner speech?" Luke asked. "I mean, besides being one you give after dinner," he joked.

The queen was about to answer when the king pretended to page through a book. "Guidebook," he mouthed.

The queen nodded and requested it from the library. "I don't see how Kirk could be ready to speak tonight," she said, shaking her head.

Kirk nodded appreciatively.

The king patted his heart as if to say, "Trust me."

When the guidebook arrived, the king took it and turned to the article on after-dinner speaking. He had Kirk read it aloud.

After-Dinner Speeches

The primary purpose of an after-dinner speech is entertainment. Although the speech should be humorous, the speaker is expected to make serious points. The speech may even be persuasive.

An excellent after-dinner speech follows these guidelines:

Introduction. Use the introduction to make a funny reference to the audience, setting, or meeting. Reference your serious **premise** and why it matters to your audience. Preview your main points.

Body. Use a variety of approaches to make your points humorously: interactive responses (ask for hands up), polls, statistics, audiovisual examples, props, demonstrations, news headlines, positive spin on negative, exaggeration, impersonations, member accomplishments, short **self-deprecating** stories, and inside jokes (only the audience understands). Avoid humor that could offend or **alienate** a group of people.

Conclusion. Review main points. Refer back to the humor in the introduction. Toast to the success of the organization or meeting, or give a call to action.

Presentation. Smile and make eye contact with the audience. A keyword outline allows you to speak more naturally. Make sure to speak slowly enough for the audience to catch the humor. Keep going confidently, even if the audience doesn't

---

> laugh. Practice with an audience before your scheduled speech if possible.

"What's a keyword outline again?" Luke asked.

The queen took the guidebook from Kirk and found an article on keywords. She read it aloud.

★ ★ ★ ★ ★ ★ ★ ★ ★ ★ ★

premise – *idea*

self-deprecating – *humble*

alienate – *turn off*

★ ★ ★ ★ ★ ★ ★ ★ ★ ★ ★

Keywords
Keywords are the most important words in a sentence or piece of writing. Taking notes of just the keywords allows a writer to recreate a story or article. For example, the first line in the fairy tale "Rumpelstiltskin" reads: Once there was a miller who was poor but had a beautiful daughter. Three of the keywords in the sentence are highlighted.   Using just the keywords in a story allows a writer to recreate it using new words and synonyms. This is good practice for beginning writers. The new sentence might be: Once upon a time, there lived an unfortunate miller who had a gorgeous daughter.   Using keywords also allows speakers to give a written speech without memorizing or reading it. The speaker can glance at the keywords and retell the main points of the speech with good eye contact.

"Too bad Kirk doesn't have a speech already written for him. He could make a keyword outline of it," Luke said.

The king clapped to get everyone's attention and nodded enthusiastically.

"You have a speech already written?" Luke asked him. When his father nodded, Kirk still looked skeptical.

"You can do it, Kirk," the queen said.

"I'm glad it's him and not me," Luke joked. When he saw the look on his mother's face, he said, "Oh, no."

"Oh, yes," the queen replied. "This is a wonderful mission for the guardians, don't you think?"

After breakfast, the king helped Kirk work on a keyword outline for his after-dinner speech. Luke and Ellen sent out a similar mission to the guardians.

What does *premise* mean?

Why should you use a keyword outline for a speech?

Why was the king confident Kirk could give the after-dinner speech for him?

Chapter 34

The queen found Ellen drawing a figure in the sunroom.

"What a beautiful character," the queen enthused. "Who is she?"

Ellen smiled. "Just a girl," she said **bashfully**.

"I know how creative you are. I'm sure you have a story to tell about this girl," the queen prodded.

★ ★ ★ ★ ★ ★ ★ ★ ★ ★

bashfully – *self-consciously*

hone – *improve*

despondently – *sadly*

★ ★ ★ ★ ★ ★ ★ ★ ★ ★

"Maybe," Ellen said, laughing. "She loves to shop. She is in the dressing room of a store and witnesses a murder. She doesn't know what to do."

"My goodness, that gives me goosebumps," the queen said. "She doesn't just report it to the police?"

"No. She's afraid that she'll be next if she does that."

"So she just walks away?"

"No. She follows the murderer."

"Now I'm really nervous!" the queen said.

Ellen giggled.

"You should work to **hone** your skill as a fiction writer. I'd like to enroll you in a writing class."

Ellen shook her head.

"What? Why wouldn't you want to improve your writing?" the queen asked.

"I want to be a better writer. But I don't want to get my hopes up about becoming a bestselling author. The odds are the same as winning the lottery," Ellen said **despondently**.

"Who told you that?" the queen said, getting irate.

"Our Grammar Girls leader. She said only one percent of published authors have any kind of success."

153

"She did, did she? I have half a mind to tell her exactly what I think of her discouragement!" the queen said angrily.

"Mother, don't. It's okay. I am just having fun," Ellen pleaded with her.

The queen was quiet for a moment. "You've raised an important issue, Ellen. Why do we learn to tell good stories? Is it just to become famous fiction authors?"

She didn't wait for Ellen to answer. Instead, she left to find Kirk and Luke. When she returned, they were with her and she had *The Guide to Grammar Galaxy* in hand.

"Luke, remember when you were learning to tell stories to the children at the library?" He nodded. "This is what you learned." She opened the guidebook and read the article titled "Storytelling."

Storytelling

Storytelling has been practiced for thousands of years. It is useful for teaching, motivating, and entertaining. Everyone tells stories, but to improve your storytelling skills, follow these steps:

Choose a story. To begin, choose a short story that you love. It could be a personal story or a story you've read. Stories that have repetitive parts are great choices. *The Three Little Pigs*'s "Then I'll huff and I'll puff and I'll blow your house in!" is an example.

Memorize the story. Make notes or use pictures of the main parts of the story and use them to tell the story after you've practiced. Keep telling the story until you can do it without notes.

Bring the story to life. Use your voice and your movements to create characters and act the story out. Use a prop or object if it adds to the story. Get your audience involved. Look them in the eye. Ask them to add the sounds to the story (like knocking) or to say repeated dialogue (like "Not by the hair of my chinny-chin-chin!").

Try it out. When you have your story ready, perform it for your family members or friends. Did you lose their interest at any point? What could you do to keep them involved in the story?

Keep telling stories and you will improve your storytelling skills.

"But storytelling involves more than dramatizing a book for young children," the queen explained. "Stories make speeches more memorable and fiction is storytelling in written form. We need to develop this skill no matter what we do for a career. Now I want to you read you the article on story writing."

Story Writing

Stories aren't just for fiction; they improve nonfiction writing as well. When including a story in nonfiction, make it short and supportive of your point. As with any good story, it must include a setting, characters, conflict, and a resolution. Make it clear what the protagonist wants and what stands in the way.

Whether you are writing a personal or fictional story, your story also needs to be written in a way that it can be experienced. Rather than *telling* what happened, *show* the reader what happened by including enough descriptive details to evoke emotion and empathy.

Telling: *The runner tripped and came in last.*

Showing: *Soon after vaulting herself from the blocks, the cleats of the runner's left shoe caught in the laces of the other shoe. She was shocked when she felt her knees and hands hit and slide along the cinder track. The pain of her scraped knees paled in comparison to the pain of disappointment she felt, limping across the finish line in last place.*

Organize a longer story with scenes. Outline the story before writing using sticky notes or storyboarding software. The setting, characters, and action may change, but each scene should move the story forward toward the resolution. Otherwise, it should be eliminated.

When you are finished writing, ask a reader to review the story for scenes that lose their interest or for dialogue that doesn't seem to fit the characters. Your story writing will improve with practice and feedback from readers.

"That last bit about practice reminds me of something. Ellen said that only one percent of authors can be considered successful. The first thing you should know is that only three percent of would-be writers publish their books. So the first obstacle to success is persisting until your book is done. The next issue is how you define success. If success is making millions writing fiction, then not many authors succeed. But if success is enjoying the writing process and delighting the people who read or hear your stories, then you'll succeed if you keep writing and seeking to improve," the queen said.

"Okay, Mother," Ellen said.

"Okay, what?" the queen asked.

"Okay, I'll sign up for the writing class," Ellen said, smiling broadly.

"I'll take it with you," the queen said. "I always want to improve in my storytelling. But first, I'd like you three to send out a mission on storytelling. It's an important skill that every guardian should develop."

The children agreed and worked on a mission with their mother's help.

What does *hone* mean?

What is the difference between telling and showing?

Why was the queen upset about what Ellen had been told concerning writing success?

Chapter 35

"Children, a new *Star Battle* movie is coming, and I have great news. You've been asked to write a review of it before it's released," the king said.

Luke groaned.

"What's the matter?" the king asked.

"I just don't expect it to be good. These sequels usually aren't," Luke said.

"I agree with you in general, but this is the *Star Battle* series we're talking about. They're always good," the king said.

"Uh, remember the last one that had no action? You were in it," Luke said.

The king reddened. "I know I was in it. It failed because of the Gremlin's dirty tricks. I'm sure this movie will be fine," he said assuredly.

"Okay," Luke said less confidently than his father.

The three English children had grown more enthusiastic by the time they were escorted into the private theater to see the new movie. The king had wanted to join them, but the director didn't want the children's opinion to be **unduly** influenced by their parents. That didn't keep the director from making sure that the royal English children had plenty of snacks, however.

★ ★ ★ ★ ★ ★ ★ ★ ★ ★

unduly – *improperly*

adhere – *stick*

cohesive – *united*

★ ★ ★ ★ ★ ★ ★ ★ ★ ★

"I love these candies, but they really **adhere** to your teeth, don't they?" Luke asked his siblings.

Ellen nodded. "I hope the princess is in this one," she said.

Kirk hushed them as the theater darkened and the film started.

The king met them outside the theater when it was over, eager to get their opinion.

"I give it a seven," Luke said.

"Hm," the king said, disappointed in the rating.

"I think that's about right," Ellen agreed.

"Kirk?" the king said to get his eldest's input.

"I agree. It was pretty good," Kirk replied.

"It sounds like you three will be able to write a **cohesive** review. Do you remember how to write with a partner? You'll write separately, edit together, and put it in one voice?" the king asked.

"Yep," Luke said dismissively.

"That gives me supreme confidence," the king joked. The children laughed.

The next week, Kirk submitted their final, edited review to the director. He thanked him for the opportunity to view the film and for the snacks.

Within an hour, the director contacted the king. "I won't be publishing your children's review," he said angrily.

"Now wait just a minute!" the king replied in kind. "You didn't tell me they were required to give a glowing review. They have to give their honest opinion. I'm sorry that they didn't like it as much as you hoped."

"That's not why I'm rejecting the review. Have you read it?" the director asked, still steaming.

"Well, of course, I—. I must admit I have not. My apologies. I will read the review and I'll get back to you," the king said, eager to end the call.

The king found his children in the castle library and asked them to show him their movie review.

"What's wrong?" Ellen asked, lips trembling. "We worked together, just as you said."

"I'll tell you after I've read your review," the king said.

The king read quietly after Kirk displayed their review on the screen. When he was finished, he sighed. "Who's your audience for this review?"

"Uh, kids?" Ellen answered hesitantly.

"So you're not sure," the king said. "Has your audience seen other *Star Battle* movies?"

"Yes? No?" Ellen guessed.

"That's one problem. I'd like to see your notes from seeing the film," the king said solemnly.

"Uh, we didn't take any," Luke admitted.

"Okay, that explains it," the king said.

"Explains what?" Kirk asked.

"Explains why the director is so unhappy with your review," the king replied. He removed *The Guide to Grammar Galaxy* from its shelf and read them articles on audience and movie reviews.

Audience
Writers and speakers have to keep their audience (the people who will read, listen to, or view their work) in mind.

Before writing, ask yourself the following questions about your audience:

How old is your audience?

Is your audience primarily male, female, or a mixture of each?

What does your audience need or what are they interested in?

How does your audience get information about your topic?

How much do they already know about your topic?

What opinions do they have on your topic?

The answers to these questions will help you inform, entertain, or persuade your audience.

Movie Reviews

A good movie review requires careful note-taking during the movie. You will want to have quotes and examples to support your opinion. You will need the title of the movie, the director's name, the lead actors' names, and the movie genre as well.

The review itself should have a title. The title of the review shares the main point of the review.

Everything is Awesome About *The Lego Movie*

Begin the review by capturing your reader's attention. Use an interesting fact, a comparison, or a **concise** opinion of the movie to **entice** the reader to continue.

If you created *The Lego Movie* at home, you would need more than 15 million legos!

The movie version of Louis Sachar's *Holes* follows the book closely.

If you choose to open your review with a comparison or fact, give your general opinion of the film next.

The creators of *The Lego Movie* have made it smart, funny, and a joy to watch.

Next, give a general plot summary without giving too much away.

Stanley, a boy cursed with bad luck, is sent to a detention camp where he and the other boys are forced to dig holes.

Then, use the examples from your note-taking to give your opinion of the plot, the acting, and other features of the film (animation, videography, editing, music, costumes, and makeup).

The opening song, "Everything is Awesome," is so catchy that kids will be singing it for weeks.

Finally, write a summary of your review. Include an explanation of which viewers are likely to enjoy the film.

The best reason to watch *Holes* is Louis Sachar's story appeals to kids and adults alike.

"Does that sound familiar?" the king asked sternly.

"Yes, sorry, Father," Ellen said. "We didn't take the review as seriously as we should have."

"How can we make up for it?" Kirk asked his father.

"I'm going to ask the director to arrange for the guardians to see the movie. Then we'll ask them to write a review for other kids who have seen *Star Battle* movies."

Ellen sniffled and the king was sorry he was so severe. "Ellen, I know your intentions were good. And it's likely to work out for the best, as most mistakes do. I'm sure the guardians could use a review on writing movie reviews for a particular audience," he said.

What does *cohesive* mean?

What do you need to know about an audience before writing or speaking?

Why do you think the director was unhappy with the children's review?

Chapter 36

"I'm excited about the change to the Annual Poetry Reading Festival this year," the queen said at breakfast.

"What change is that? I haven't heard about it," the king said.

"All poems will be original. The children will be writing them!" she said with enthusiasm.

"I can certainly see some benefit to that," the king said.

"Yes. I know the children will enjoy it," she said, looking at Kirk, Luke, and Ellen.

But she was met with sullen faces and plates of uneaten food.

"What's wrong? Are you ill?" she asked, suddenly concerned.

"I'm fine, but I'm not a poet," Luke said.

"Me either," Kirk agreed.

"I've written poetry, but it's not my thing," Ellen said.

The queen was stunned. "I'm surprised at your attitudes."

"Do we have to do it?" Luke whined.

"I'd prefer not to," Kirk agreed.

"I know I'm never going to be poet laureate," Ellen joked to lighten the mood.

The king stroked his beard, thinking. "I see that you children are not **keen** to participate in the festival. You do work very hard serving this galaxy. Therefore, I think it would be acceptable for you to **abstain** from participating this year."

⋆ ⋆ ⋆ ⋆ ⋆ ⋆ ⋆ ⋆ ⋆ ⋆

keen – *eager*

abstain – *withdraw*

regained – *recovered*

⋆ ⋆ ⋆ ⋆ ⋆ ⋆ ⋆ ⋆ ⋆ ⋆

The three children cheered. Ellen jumped up to hug her father. When she sat down again, all three siblings **regained** their appetites and began eating their breakfast eagerly.

It was the queen's turn to be sullen and have no appetite.

"What is it, dear?" the king asked.

"I would think you would consult me before making that decision," she said, her face reddening in anger.

"Well, I didn't realize you felt so strongly about it. It's just one poetry festival," the king said, shrugging.

"That's right, Mother. We can participate another year," Luke said.

"But will you?" the queen asked, her throat hoarse with emotion. "Please excuse me," she said, leaving the table abruptly.

When she had gone, Ellen said what they were all thinking. "Uh-oh."

"Why is it so important to her?" Kirk asked.

"Wait. Isn't it scheduled for Mother's Day weekend?" Ellen suggested.

"That's it! I wasn't thinking. She loves the festival. I'll tell her that we'll go, even if you three aren't reading," the king said, sure he had found a solution.

Later the king found his wife in their bedchamber, still upset. "I know why you're so emotional about this," he said, putting his arm around her.

"You do?" she asked, sniffling.

"Yes. The festival is Mother's Day weekend and you love it. We're all committed to going with you." He smiled and hugged her.

The queen frowned and pushed herself away. "That's not what I was hoping you'd say."

"What is it then?" he asked.

"I'm surprised at you, allowing the children to skip something just because they don't think they're good at it. How can they become good poets if they don't practice? And how will they learn to enjoy it if they don't become good at it?" she asked.

The king sat quietly, thinking. "You're right," he said.

"Could you say that again? I heard you, but I like the sound of it," she joked.

The king laughed. "I'm off to give the children the bad news," he said with a smile. "It will be a gift to you to have them participate, but it will be an even bigger gift to them. Writing poetry is enjoyable when you practice. You're right as usual," he said, kissing her on the forehead.

The king found the children in the sunroom and explained their mother's thinking on the festival. They nodded in agreement. "I think participating is not only a good idea for you but for the guardians as

163

well," he said. "Let's review poetry writing in the guidebook, and then I'll have you send out a mission."

Writing Poetry

Writing poetry begins with reading plenty of poetry and listening to it read aloud. Committing poems to memory will also improve your poetry writing.

First, choose a topic for your poem. Then choose the type of poem to write. If you're a beginning poetry writer, start with a small poem like a haiku or cinquain. A haiku is a three-line, unrhymed poem that usually has a nature theme. The first and third lines have five syllables, while the second has seven. A cinquain is also a five-line poem with two, four, six, eight, and two syllables respectively.

Choose to write a descriptive or narrative poem. A descriptive poem relies on sensory language and literary devices that communicate a lot with few words. A thesaurus is useful in choosing quality adjectives and adverbs for this type of poetry. Make a list of all the words that describe your topic before you begin writing your first draft.

Narrative poems have a setting, characters, and a plot just as stories do. Make a list of strong vocabulary words that describe each part of your story before writing.

Choose to write a rhyming or free-verse poem. Rhyming poetry follows a rhyme scheme. A common scheme is ABAB in which the last words of alternating lines rhyme. Rhyme does not have to be exact, so a slant rhyme like cut/hat is acceptable. A rhyming dictionary helps identify rhyming words. A limerick is a short (five-line), rhyming, narrative poem with an AABBA rhyming format.

A free-verse poem does not have a rhyme scheme or a syllable requirement. One unique form of free-verse poetry is written using words clipped from periodicals or using word magnets.

After writing, read your poem aloud to help you edit it.

What does *keen* mean?

What is a free-verse poem?

Why was the queen upset?

About the Author

Dr. Melanie Wilson was a clinical psychologist working in a Christian practice, a college instructor, freelance writer, and public speaker before she felt called to stay home and educate her children. She is a mother of six and has homeschooled for more than 20 years. She says it's her most fulfilling vocation.

Melanie has always been passionate about language arts and used bits and pieces of different curriculum and approaches to teach her children and friends' children. In 2014, she believed she had another calling to write the curriculum she had always wanted as a homeschooling mom — one that didn't take a lot of time, made concepts simple and memorable, and was enough fun to keep her kids motivated.

Books have been a family business since the beginning. Melanie's husband Mark has been selling library books for over 30 years. Melanie and the older kids frequently pitch in to help at the annual librarians' conference. Grammar Galaxy is another family business that has been another great learning opportunity for their children.

When Melanie isn't busy homeschooling, visiting her kids in college, or writing, she loves to play tennis with family and friends.

Melanie is also the author of *The Organized Homeschool Life, A Year of Living Productively,* and *So You're Not Wonder Woman.* Learn more on her blog, Psychowith6.com, and her podcast, HomeschoolSanity.com.

About the Illustrator

Rebecca Mueller has had an interest in drawing from an early age. Rebecca quickly developed a unique style and illustrated her first books, a short series of bedtime stories with her mother, at age 9. Rebecca graduated with a BA in English from the University of Missouri - St. Louis with a minor in Studio Art and her Master of Library and Information Science at the University of Missouri – Columbia. She currently works as a Youth Specialist at the St. Louis Public Library.

Appendix: Answers to Comprehension Questions

Chapter 1
What does *unyielding* mean? inflexible

What is a literary genre? A literary genre is a category of writing based on style, content, length, or intended audience.

Why does the head librarian want to archive some genres? To make room for more popular titles.

Chapter 2
What does *unyielding* mean? inflexible

What are two types of figurative language? Similes, metaphors, personification, idioms, allusion, synecdoche, metonymy

Why were figures of speech coming to life? The Figurative Language Festival was being held in Nonfiction Province.

Chapter 3
What does *piqued* mean? annoyed

What are myths?
Myths are the oldest form of fictional stories. They have been told and passed down to explain creation or natural events.

Why did people on the boat tour see what they thought were amazing special effects? Greek Mythology was moved to Nonfiction Province.

Chapter 4
What does *ensuing* mean? following

What is a story arc? The sequence of events in the plot

Why did a chimera appear on stage? It was in Nonfiction Province on planet Composition.

Chapter 5

What does *undermine* mean? weaken

What is a plot feature that contributes to character change? Loss or failure; entering a new world; needs being met

Why doesn't the king think the Gremlin has changed? He is still critical of the king and isn't taking full responsibility for his choices.

Chapter 6

What does *procure* mean? get

What is a round-robin reading in Readers Theatre? Each student reads a character's lines before passing the script to the next student.

Why was the king upset with the leaders of Grammar Girls and Grammar Guys? He thought the leaders weren't serious about doing quality theater.

Chapter 7

What does *erudite* mean? intellectual

Which should be read first in a reading-comprehension test—the passage or questions? The passage.

Why does the queen suspect the Gremlin of producing the test tips Kirk found? Because they will lead to poor scores.

Chapter 8

What does *ruse* mean? scam

What are glittering generalities? Vague, positive phrases used to win an audience's support.

Why was the king upset? He knew some citizens would believe lies about him.

<u>Chapter 9</u>
What does *trite* mean? corny

What do reviews need to be taken seriously? proper grammar, spelling, and vocabulary

Why does the king suspect the Gremlin wrote the review of *Too Many Cooks in the Kitchen*? It's negative and anonymous.

<u>Chapter 10</u>
What does *elude* mean? escape

Why is vocabulary important? Better communication and you're more likely to be successful

What had led to the children's weaker vocabulary? Not using their word books and bad habits of using weak vocabulary.

<u>Chapter 11</u>
What does *preempt* mean? prevent

Do you remember what a prefix and suffix are? Both are word parts that change a word's meaning. A prefix comes before a root word and a suffix comes after.

Do you agree with the queen's approach to Prefix & Suffix? Why or why not?

<u>Chapter 12</u>
What does *befuddled* mean? confused

What is wrong with Luke's Most Highest Jumper award? The word most shouldn't be included.

When an adjective is a single syllable, which comparative and superlative should be used? -er/-est

Chapter 13
What does *raucous* mean? loud

Why is it important to have synonyms? They keep writing from becoming repetitive.

What was the king planning to say to the director of the Thesaurus Office? S/he was fired, and the unity initiative was canceled.

Chapter 14
What does *precarious* mean? dangerous

What does TBD mean? To be determined

Why was the king suspicious of the new judge? No one had heard of him and he gave Acronym the golden buzzer.

Chapter 15
What does *arbitrary* mean? random

What word uses the spelling rule i before e except after c or when ei says /ay/as in neighbor and weigh?
friend, believe, relief

Why does the ABC1 bill sponsor want to eliminate spelling rules?
Because spelling hasn't improved.

Chapter 16
What does *tentatively* mean in the story? hesitantly

Why did the queen suggest allowing the homophone-spelling bill to pass?
So people would learn the importance of correct homophone spelling.

Why was there a meat shortage in the galaxy?
Single people were going to meat counters to meet people and left with meat.

Chapter 17
What does *solidify* mean? strengthen

Why was the king concerned about misspelled words being featured in media? It would make continued misspellings more likely.

What is one of the misspelled words on the top 100 list? embarass, congradulate, privelege, succesful

Chapter 18
What does *undisclosed* mean? secret

When are the words *city* and *county* capitalized? When they are part of the city/county name

What should you do when you're confused about capitalization? Do an Internet search

Chapter 19
What is a ransom? payoff

Why was Ellen's toothbrush missing? It's a noun and nouns were disappearing.

What is an irregular plural noun? It does not form the plural with -s or -es

Chapter 20
What does *acquiesced* mean? agreed

What information does a helping verb often give about the main verb? When action occurred

Why was everyone in the castle tired? The Verb Freedom Act allowed active verbs to be inactive.

Chapter 21
What does *demeaned* mean? humiliated

What is an object of a preposition? A noun or pronoun at the end of a prepositional phrase.

Which prepositions do you tend to forget?

Chapter 22
What does *oblivion* mean? nothingness

What is a compound predicate? Two or more verbs with the same subject.

Does the king's mother like to care for her grandchildren? No.

Chapter 23
What does *quaint* mean? Old-fashioned

What is an example of an irregular verb? Make, say, do, etc.

Why didn't the queen want screens on the trip? She wanted to have undistracted family time.

Chapter 24
What does *impudent* mean? disrespectful

What part of speech is the word *bad*? adjective

Why was the dentist using improper grammar? Adverbs were living near nouns, and adjectives were living near verbs.

Chapter 25
What does *succumbed* mean? surrendered

Which type of pronoun do compound subjects take?
Plural

Why were pronouns unusable during the family's bowling game?
They weren't working while they waited for an agent to negotiate for them.

Chapter 26
What does *forlorn* mean? sad

Do possessive pronouns include apostrophes? No.

Why should viewers be suspicious of the professor's opinion on possessive nouns and pronouns? His name means chaos.

Chapter 27

What does *twaddle* mean? nonsense

When should you use a single quotation mark? When a quote is used within a quote.

Which rule did Inky break in punctuating the sentence I need help? She used quotes for emphasis instead of for expressing doubt.

Chapter 28

What does *favor* mean? Approval

What does dictation teach? Writing speed, spelling, and grammar

Why was the children's writing so slow? Speed drills on planet Spelling were exhausting the letters.

Chapter 29

What does *distinctive* mean? unique

What should you do if you've said a sentence poorly while using dictation software? Speak the sentence correctly a second time.

Why should the king have been suspicious about the company providing the software? The company name means suspicious.

Chapter 30

What does *diffidently* mean? self-consciously

What should happen to your tone when coming to the end of a sentence you are reading aloud? It should drop.

Why did the king think the Gremlin was at fault for Luke's slow reading? He didn't want to hurt Luke's feelings by blaming him.

Chapter 31

What does *circumspectly* mean? cautiously

What five things are required for a complete sentence?
A capital letter, end mark, subject, verb, complete thought.

Why was the queen concerned about Ellen's new friendship with Alexis? Alexis wasn't friendly to the queen and Ellen's behavior changed.

Chapter 32
What does *floated* mean in the story? proposed

What is the topic sentence of an essay exam response called? Thesis statement

What does the king think is behind Parliament's idea of dismantling the guardian program? The Gremlin

Chapter 33
What does *premise* mean? idea

Why should you use a keyword outline for a speech? It doesn't require memorization and allows for good eye contact.

Why was the king confident Kirk could give the after-dinner speech for him? He already had the speech written and Kirk could use keywords to deliver it.

Chapter 34
What does *hone* mean? improve

What is the difference between telling and showing? Telling explains what happened; showing includes enough descriptive details to evoke emotion and empathy.

Why was the queen upset about what Ellen had been told concerning writing success? She wanted her to keep writing and not to be discouraged.

Chapter 35
What does *cohesive* mean? united

What do you need to know about an audience before writing or speaking? Age, gender, needs, interests, information sources, topic familiarity, opinions

174

Why do you think the director was unhappy with the children's review? They didn't consider the audience or use tips for writing a good review.

Chapter 36
What does *keen* mean? eager

What is a free-verse poem? It does not have a rhyme scheme or syllable requirement.

Why was the queen upset? She didn't want the children not writing poetry because they didn't think they were good at it.

Made in the USA
Monee, IL
02 July 2021